D0093944

THE ULTIMATE CATHOLIC QUIZ

Karl Keating

THE ULTIMATE CATHOLIC QUIZ

100 Questions Most Catholics Can't Answer

IGNATIUS PRESS   SAN FRANCISCO

Cover design by Devin Schadt, Saint Louis Creative

© 2016 by Karl Keating
All rights reserved
Published in 2016 by Ignatius Press, San Francisco
ISBN 978-1-62164-024-0
Library of Congress Control Number 2015930776
Printed in the United States of America ⊗

For Teruko

WELCOME!

How well do you know Catholic teachings, practices, and history? You're about to find out.

In the following pages, I offer for your amusement one hundred questions. Each is followed by five possible answers. Only one of the answers is completely correct. It's your task to find it. It won't be as easy as you might imagine. You will have difficulty in winnowing the answers. Some questions will stump you completely, and you'll be reduced to making a random guess. As a concession to those who are easily discouraged, for a few questions I have proposed one or even two glaringly wrong answers. You should be able to spot them immediately. (If you can't, go ahead and feel discouraged.)

There are no trick questions, but there are questions that will trip you up if you fail to read carefully. Words are used precisely and not necessarily in the colloquial sense. An answer is counted as wrong if any part of it—such as a date or a name—is wrong. Your goal is not to find the answer that is least wrong but the one answer that is wholly right, which may be "none of the above".

This quiz does not pretend to be comprehensive. It has only one hundred questions, after all, so most matters of Catholic belief and practice aren't mentioned. Still, the questions cover multiple areas—doctrines, morals, customs, history, personalities—and should provide your mind with a good workout. You likely will find areas of strength and weakness in your knowledge. You might answer all the doctrine questions correctly, but none of the history questions. Or the other way around. None of us is omnicompetent.

I tested some of these questions with groups of intelligent, well-educated Catholics. It may console you to know that never did anyone in those groups find all of the correct answers, and most people found only about half. With that in mind, I suggest that you not reveal to anyone that you're taking this quiz until you learn whether your score merits cheers or jeers.

As you take the quiz, record your answers on a sheet of paper. An answer key is provided at the back of the book along with a scoring scale.

I

The Ark of the Covenant

a. was built by Noah.

b. housed the tablets of the law.

c. was burned piece by piece by Caiaphas.

d. probably never existed; it was made up to instruct the Israelites about Yahweh's mercy.

e. none of the above

a. The Ark of the Covenant wasn't a boat. You will find the account of the Flood, and thus Noah's ark (a very large boat), in Genesis 6–9.

b. Yes. It was more like a safe-deposit box, made of gold-plated wood and measuring two and a half cubits in length and one and a half cubits in width and height. (A cubit is the length from the elbow to the tip of the outstretched middle finger, about eighteen inches.)

c. It was lost centuries before Caiaphas was born. The Babylonians destroyed Jerusalem and Solomon's Temple in 597 B.C., and there is no record of the Ark's location after that. According to the ancient Jewish historian Josephus, Caiaphas was appointed high priest in A.D. 18.

d. If some adventurous biblical scholar has suggested this, I've missed the news—and, if he has suggested it, he's wrong.

e. The right answer is *b*.

2

The patron of air travelers is

    a. Saint Frances of Rome.

    b. Sister Bertrille, the flying nun.

    c. Saint Joseph of Cupertino.

    d. Saint Bona of Pisa.

    e. none of the above.

a. In 1925 Pope Pius XI named Frances of Rome the patron saint of automobile drivers. His choice derived from the legend that when Frances walked along roads at night, an angel lighted her way with a lantern so that she would not stumble.

b. Sister Bertrille was the name of the main character in the television show *The Flying Nun*, which ran from 1967 to 1970. She "flew" when a breeze caught her large, stiff cornette and lifted her off the ground.

c. Joseph of Cupertino (1603–1663) was a Franciscan friar and mystic known to levitate when in deep prayer, an accomplishment sufficiently impressive for him to be named patron of air travelers, aviators, and astronauts.

d. Bona of Pisa (1156–1207) almost qualifies. She is the patron saint of travelers in general and specifically of guides, pilgrims, and flight attendants—but not of air travelers as such.

e. Answer *c* is correct.

3

Who committed the first sin, not counting the fallen angels?

a. Cain, when he murdered his brother Abel

b. Adam, from whom we inherit original sin

c. Eve, from whom we inherit original sin

d. Adam and Eve together, from whom we inherit original sin

e. none of the above

a. No, since Adam and Eve had sinned even before Cain and Abel were born.

b. No, because Eve sinned before Adam when she ate the forbidden fruit. His sin came immediately thereafter. See Genesis 3:6.

c. Although Eve sinned first and induced Adam to sin, we do not inherit original sin from her but from him, because he was the head of the human race.

d. No, since we don't inherit original sin from Eve.

e. Each of the above answers is incorrect, making this one the right answer.

4

A priest's power to confect the Eucharist

    a. comes through the people present at Mass; thus, a congregation is needed for a Mass to be valid.

    b. is less than a bishop's power, but greater than a deacon's power, to confect the Eucharist.

    c. is given to him through the laying on of hands by his ordaining bishop.

    d. was not taught by Vatican II, which recognized that the Eucharist is not confected but is made present spiritually.

    e. none of the above

a. How can this be, since a private Mass by a priest is not only valid but encouraged? A priest doesn't need a congregation to celebrate a valid Mass; he doesn't even need an altar server.

b. When it comes to the Eucharist, bishops and priests have exactly the same consecrating power. A deacon has none.

c. This is correct.

d. Vatican II said no such thing. If it had, it would have contradicted infallible teaching—an impossibility.

e. The correct answer is *c*.

5

What is circumincession?

    a. the ancient Jewish initiatory rite for male children

    b. the indwelling of each Person of the Trinity in the others

    c. the manner in which the New World was divided up between Spain and Portugal

    d. a manner of procession used by concelebrating priests

    e. none of the above

a. No, you're thinking of circumcision.

b. Yes, this is right. Also known by the Greek term *perichoresis*, *circumincession* can be spelled as *circuminsession*. The late Father John Hardon, S.J., defined *circumincession* this way: "The mutual immanence of the three distinct persons of the Holy Trinity. The Father is entirely in the Son, likewise in the Holy Spirit; and so is the Son in the Father and the Holy Spirit; and the Holy Spirit in the Father and the Son" (*Modern Catholic Dictionary*, Doubleday, 1980, pp. 106-7).

c. Not even close. Perhaps you heard an echo of *circumnavigation* and so guessed that circumincession had something to do with explorations.

d. If you chose this answer, perhaps you had in mind something to do with a liturgical procession.

e. Answer *b* is correct.

6

The Rosary

    a. was invented by Saint Dominic.

    b. is making a comeback among both Catholics and Protestants.

    c. is necessary for salvation; you can't be considered a good Catholic without at least occasionally praying the Rosary.

    d. was prayed weekly by Pope Saint John XXIII.

    e. none of the above

a. Many people think so, but the Rosary predated Saint Dominic. Centuries before him, monks had begun to recite all 150 psalms together in choir. As time went on, it was felt that lay brothers, known as *conversi*, should have some form of prayer of their own. They were distinct from choir monks, and a chief distinction was that they were illiterate. Since they couldn't read the psalms, they couldn't recite them with the monks. They needed an easily remembered prayer. The prayer first chosen was the Our Father. The *conversi* used strings of beads to keep count of the prayers. During the twelfth century, those beads came to be used to count Hail Marys—or, more properly, the first half of what we now call the Hail Mary (the second half was added later).

b. True. The comeback is obvious among Catholics, but now even some Protestants are turning to the Rosary. (Mr. Ripley, call your office.)

c. Incorrect. Although praying the Rosary is a good thing, you needn't suffer pangs of conscience if it happens not to be your favorite devotion. There is no obligation to pray it.

d. Before he was elected pope, Angelo Roncalli prayed five decades of the Rosary daily, but after his election as John XXIII, he went to the full fifteen traditional decades, saying to an inquirer, "Now that I'm pope, I need more help."

e. This is incorrect because *b* is the right answer.

7

Angels

    a. are whiskerless youths.

    b. are fat babies with wings.

    c. don't have to be believed in.

    d. are referred to, but not explicitly, in the Nicene Creed.

    e. none of the above

a. Only in paintings are angels youths.

b. Angels are not babies either. Fortunately, this Baroque artistic convention no longer is in use. It may have helped to give rise to the popular idea that, when an infant dies, he becomes an angel in heaven. This is quite wrong. Men and angels are distinct kinds of creatures. One can't turn into the other. When a human being of any age dies and goes to heaven, he is in heaven as a human being—initially just as a soul, later (at the end of time) with his resurrected body. Granted, human souls are spirits, and angels are spirits, but they are quite different spirits. (God is a spirit too, and he is immeasurably more different still.) A yet-bodiless man in heaven is not an angel and should not be referred to as one, even colloquially.

c. Of course you have to believe in angels.

d. The Nicene Creed recited on Sundays refers to believing in "all things visible and invisible" (in Latin, "visibilium omnium et invisibilium"). The unseen or invisible part of creation includes good angels and fallen angels (demons).

e. Answer *d* is right.

8

The Catholic Church is

    a. one of several churches established by Christ.

    b. part of the original Christian Church, the other parts being Eastern Orthodox churches and Protestant churches.

    c. the only ecclesial body in which the Church founded by Christ subsists.

    d. closest sacramentally to the Anglican, then to the Eastern Orthodox, and lastly to the Protestant churches.

    e. none of the above.

a. Christ established only one Church. See Matthew 16:18: "[Y]ou are Peter, and on this rock I will build my Church." Notice that *Church* is in the singular. Christ didn't say, "I will build several churches."

b. The original Church didn't split into coequal parts. The Eastern Orthodox went into schism (commonly reckoned from 1054), and Protestants split off and developed new doctrines of their own (1517 and after).

c. Yes. Vatican II says that Jesus' Church "subsists" in the Catholic Church (*Lumen Gentium*, 8). This means that the Catholic Church is the only place that Jesus' Church is found in her fullness, even though elements of sanctification and true teaching can be found in other ecclesial communions—for example, valid baptism and correct teaching on the factuality of the Resurrection. The use of the word *subsists* in no way contradicts earlier teaching, such as that by Pope Pius XII in 1950, when he stated that "the Mystical Body of Christ and the Roman Catholic Church are one and the same thing" (*Humani Generis*, 27).

d. We're closer sacramentally to the Eastern Orthodox, who have valid priestly orders and thus all seven sacraments, than to Anglicans and other Protestants, who don't have valid orders and thus have only two valid sacraments, baptism and matrimony (the two that don't require the ministration of a priest).

e. Answer *c* is correct.

9

Christ first knew he was God

    a. at the presentation in the Temple, when his divinity was recognized by the holy man Simeon (Lk 2:29–32).

    b. on the cross, when the Father's purpose was revealed fully as Christ said, "It is finished" (Jn 19:30).

    c. at the finding in the Temple, when the twelve-year-old Jesus said, "I must be about my Father's business" (Lk 2:49, King James Version).

    d. when the apostle Thomas, the doubter, saw the risen Christ and cried out, "My Lord and my God!" (Jn 20:28).

    e. none of the above

a. Nothing in this Gospel account indicates that the infant Christ first realized his divinity when Simeon saw him.

b. Some modern writers claim that it was only in the last moments of his life that Christ came to know who he really was. Nothing in the accounts of the Crucifixion suggests that.

c. One could argue that at least by this time, when the young Jesus was found in the Temple and said to Mary and Joseph that he was there because he was doing his Father's business, he must have known who he was—but that merely suggests that he knew no later than that incident, not that he first came to know his real identity then.

d. Think of the sequence here. Christ already had suffered, died, and risen from the grave. How could he not have known of his divinity? If he first came to know it only when Thomas saw him days after the Resurrection, who did Jesus imagine himself to be between the Resurrection and the meeting with Thomas?

e. The other answers are incorrect. Here is the right answer: It is enough to realize that in Jesus Christ there are two natures (divine and human) but only one Person. That Person is the Second Person of the Trinity and therefore God. When we ask, "When did Jesus first know he was God?" we're asking, "When did this Person first know he was God?" It is a person (whether divine, angelic, or human) who knows, not a nature. Since God always has known he is God, the divine Person whom we call Jesus Christ (God the Son) always has known himself to be God. Since persons know according to their natures, we can distinguish the Second Person of the Trinity's knowledge of himself as God by means of his divine nature from what he knew about himself by means of his human nature. By means of his divine nature, he has always known himself to be God, even if in his human nature (his human manner of knowing) this would not always have been the case.

IO

How many miraculous cures at Lourdes has the Church recognized officially?

- a. none, since Lourdes is a place of pilgrimage
- b. only the cure of Saint Bernadette Soubirous, the visionary at Lourdes
- c. more than eight hundred, which is a tiny fraction of the cures claimed by the millions of people who have visited Lourdes
- d. fewer than seventy
- e. none of the above

a. Lourdes indeed is a place of pilgrimage, with about five million pilgrims and tourists visiting each year, but that status hardly disqualifies it from being a place where miraculous cures have occurred. After all, the claim of miracles is what draws most of the pilgrims. Had no miracles been alleged to have occurred, no doubt visitors would be far fewer.

b. Bernadette was not herself cured of an illness.

c. Over the years, Lourdes has seen millions of pilgrims, a good portion of whom sought a cure for their illnesses. How many left Lourdes with an improvement that, in its apparent impossibility, would qualify as a miracle? We don't know, but the number likely is much larger than the number of officially recognized miracles. Could it be as large as eight hundred? Maybe, but there is no way to tell. (Most healings at Lourdes are said to be not of the physical but of the emotional or moral sort, which are very great things in themselves.)

d. The Lourdes Medical Bureau is charged with evaluating claims of miraculous cures. About three dozen cases are brought to its attention yearly, and almost all of those are dismissed at once. A few are investigated thoroughly, and usually none of them passes muster. As of this writing, only sixty-seven cures have been certified by the bureau as miraculous.

e. The correct answer is *d*.

II

Which of the following is *not* a pairing of one of the seven deadly sins with an opposite virtue?

a. gluttony and temperance
b. wrath and kindness
c. avarice and charity
d. sloth and diligence
e. none of the above

a. The list of seven deadly sins, as we have it now, seems to have been more or less finalized by Pope Gregory I around 590. He gave them as lust, gluttony, avarice (greed), sloth, anger (wrath), envy, and pride. This is the order in which they are repeated in Dante's *Divine Comedy*, though the *Catechism of the Catholic Church* lists them in this order: pride, avarice, envy, wrath, lust, gluttony, and sloth. Each of these sins has a corresponding and contrary virtue that, if cultivated, will help to keep one from committing the sin. The contrary virtue to gluttony is temperance, so answer *a* is not the right answer to the question.

b. Wrath (also called anger) has as its contrary virtue patience, not kindness, though kindness in some ways seems to be appropriate too. It's hard to be angry toward someone to whom you're being kind. Nevertheless, the correct contrary virtue to wrath is patience, so this pairing is incorrect, which makes this the right answer.

c. Charity indeed is the contrary virtue to avarice (greed).

d. Diligence is the contrary virtue to sloth.

e. Answer *b* is correct.

12

The Communion Host may be received

    a. on the tongue only if the church has an altar rail.

    b. either on the tongue or in the hand, as per the preference of the individual communicant.

    c. whichever way the majority of the parishioners may vote.

    d. only as the pastor determines, after consulting with the parish council.

    e. none of the above

a. Apparently you haven't been in any rail-less churches lately. Altar rails certainly are a convenience for those who wish to receive Communion on the tongue while kneeling, but they are not required. You may receive on the tongue while kneeling in the absence of an altar rail (it's called kneeling on the cold, hard floor) or while standing.

b. Yes. On the tongue is the normative or standard way; in the hand is the optional way. The April 1999 issue of *Notitiae*, the official publication of the Congregation for Divine Worship, stated that "the right to receive the Eucharistic bread on the tongue still remains intact to the faithful."

c. Wrong. Even if everyone else votes for in the hand, you may receive on the tongue, and if everyone else votes for on the tongue, you may receive in the hand (at least at Masses in the Ordinary Form; in the Extraordinary Form, reception is always on the tongue).

d. Still wrong. Neither the pastor nor the parish council has the authority to decide. The choice is yours.

e. The correct answer is *b*.

13

The *Catechism of the Catholic Church*

    a. is intended to be used exclusively by bishops.

    b. is intended to be used by bishops, priests, and religious educators only.

    c. takes effect in a particular country only when that country's national bishops' conference approves it.

    d. is intended to be used by lay Catholics.

    e. none of the above

a. That's not what John Paul II said when he promulgated the *Catechism of the Catholic Church* in 1992.

b. He didn't say that either.

c. The *Catechism* doesn't need the approval of national bishops' conferences.

d. Bingo. The *Catechism* is for use by every Catholic, including laypeople.

e. The right answer is right above.

1

Apologetics

    a. is part of evangelization.

    b. is a word we no longer use in polite company.

    c. means apologizing for the sins Catholics committed against our separated brethren over the centuries.

    d. involves using any means necessary to get non-Catholics to admit that they're wrong.

    e. none of the above

a. Apologetics is the narrower word, evangelization the wider; the latter can be said to include the former. We can think of apologetics as getting people ready for evangelization by helping them to overcome misconceptions, prejudices, and lack of understanding. Apologetics softens 'em up, and evangelization closes in for the conversion.

b. Maybe it is according to some people, but not in the opinion of the enlightened.

c. *Apologetics* is not a synonym for *apologizing*—at least not in the saying "I'm sorry" sense. The word *apologetics* comes from Latin and Greek terms that mean to give a defense or an explanation of something.

d. Some people may think so, but if you take that attitude, you'll fail as an apologist. Apologetics often includes argumentation—the calm, reasoned, and charitable discussion of differences. It doesn't include picking up your opponent by the lapels and trying to shake sense into him.

e. The correct answer is *a*.

15

Women someday will be ordained as priests

    a. because in the ancient Church there were women priests.

    b. because in the ancient Church there were women deacons.

    c. most likely after the next ecumenical council. .

    d. In fact, they won't be ordained.

    e. none of the above

a. There were no women priests in the ancient Church—or at any other time in the Church's history.

b. Yes, there were "deaconesses" in the early Church, but they were not ordained and were not female equivalents of male deacons. They were something like today's nuns, generally older women (often widows) who were deputed to perform charitable tasks, such as looking after the poor and the ill.

c. Wishful thinking and poor theology. An ecumenical council can teach infallibly matters of faith or morals, but it can't undo what already has been taught infallibly, whether by another ecumenical council, by a pope, or by the universal teaching of the Church. In his 1994 apostolic letter *Ordinatio Sacerdotalis* (*Priestly Ordination*) John Paul II reiterated the Church's perennial teaching that the ministerial priesthood is reserved to males only. He said, "We declare that the Church has no authority whatsoever to confer priestly ordination on women and that this judgment is to be definitively held by all the Church's faithful." Although *Ordinatio Sacerdotalis* was not itself an exercise in the extraordinary papal Magisterium, its contents are infallible by virtue of always having been taught by the ordinary Magisterium of the Church. This was confirmed in 1998 in a document from the Congregation for the Doctrine of the Faith, then headed by Joseph Cardinal Ratzinger, the future Benedict XVI, who wrote that the teaching already had "been set forth infallibly by the ordinary and universal Magisterium", even before the issuance of *Ordinatio Sacerdotalis*.

d. True, women will never be ordained. The issue really is closed, no matter how much some people insist on talking about it.

e. The correct answer is *d*.

16

Vatican City

    a. is a separate country located entirely inside the city of Rome.

    b. is part of Italy, but has federal administrative status according to the 1929 concordat between the Vatican and the Italian government.

    c. may be willed by a pope to his heirs, even though no pope has ever used that prerogative.

    d. is the third-smallest country in the world.

    e. none of the above

a. Correct.

b. Although surrounded by Italy, Vatican City State is a separate state. It was the Lateran Treaty of 1929 that formalized this fact.

c. If you marked this answer, go to your room. The only things modern popes have owned, and therefore have been in a position to pass along to their heirs (commonly brothers and sisters, nephews and nieces) are a few personal effects. Popes have no ownership interest in any of the buildings or artworks located in Vatican City or, for that matter, overseen by the Church anywhere else in the world.

d. The third smallest country is Andorra, the second is San Marino, and the first is Vatican City.

e. The right answer is *a*.

17

What is the breviary?

    a. an abbreviated form of the New Testament

    b. the Latin-rite variant of an aviary

    c. the readings of the Divine Office, all set to music

    d. a book containing prayers, hymns, psalms, and readings for the canonical hours

    e. none of the above

a. It isn't clear what an abbreviated form of the New Testament would be called, other than brief, but "breviary" isn't it.

b. If you chose this answer, open your dictionary to *aviary*.

c. Close, since the breviary, which is commonly called the Divine Office or Liturgy of the Hours, contains hymns, but mostly it contains prayers that are not set to music.

d. Bingo. The term *breviary* comes from the Latin *brevis*, which means short or concise—like this answer.

e. Look right above.

18

Holy Communion may be received by

   a. anyone at all, so long as his conscience tells him it is the right thing to do.

   b. any Christian who wishes to manifest the unity that Christ willed for his Church.

   c. Catholics in the state of grace, but not by most Protestants, even if they are in the state of grace.

   d. Catholics who have committed mortal sins and are sorry for them, even if they have not confessed them yet in confession.

   e. none of the above.

a. Wrong, because, as an obvious case, non-Christians may not receive Communion, nor may someone knowingly do so in the state of mortal sin.

b. No, because canon law provides that only those Christians (such as the Eastern Orthodox) who believe in the Real Presence as Catholics do may receive Communion in Catholic churches (canon 844). All they need to do is ask.

c. Correct. Since most Protestants do not believe as Catholics do regarding the Real Presence, they may not receive Communion, even if they are in the state of grace. The very act of receiving Communion is a visible sign that you believe exactly as the Catholic Church teaches concerning the Real Presence, and most Protestants don't.

d. Close, but no. Absent a life-or-death situation, you must go to confession before receiving Communion, even if you have repented of your mortal sin.

e. Answer *c* is correct.

19

Creation means

    a. God made everything out of nothing.

    b. God made everything out of unformed plasmatic matter.

    c. God made everything out of empty space.

    d. God set the universe in motion and then withdrew.

    e. none of the above.

a. Creation refers to God's making everything without pre-existing things of any sort. Things are literally made out of "no thing", or nothing.

b. Even plasmatic (unformed, chaotic) matter is a thing, a kind of matter.

c. Even empty space is a thing—an empty thing, but still a thing. This answer and answer *b* are popular with some present-day cosmologists. They speak in terms of the universe being made out of nothing, but by "nothing" they actually mean a very low-level something. True nothingness is the absence of absolutely everything.

d. This has nothing to do with creation one way or the other. The idea that God got things going and then took off is known as Deism. It is a theological position historically popular with those who wish to acknowledge God's role in setting things up but not his role in keeping things going or in promulgating commands by which we are expected to live—especially the latter.

e. There is nothing wrong with answer *a*.

20

Ecumenical councils

a. are always held at the Vatican.

b. have their acts ratified by the pope—that's what makes them ecumenical.

c. are invalid unless attended by an absolute majority of the world's bishops.

d. have been held sixteen times, the latest being Vatican II.

e. none of the above

a. Only two have been held at the Vatican.

b. Precisely. The pope does not need to be in attendance; sometimes only his legates are.

c. There is no numerical requirement. A council is ecumenical if the pope says so, even if only a minority of the world's bishops are able to attend.

d. There have been twenty-one ecumenical councils so far:

1. Nicaea I (325)
2. Constantinople I (381)
3. Ephesus (431)
4. Chalcedon (451)
5. Constantinople II (553)
6. Constantinople III (680–681)
7. Nicaea II (787)
8. Constantinople IV (869–870)
9. Lateran I (1123)
10. Lateran II (1139)
11. Lateran III (1179)
12. Lateran IV (1215)
13. Lyon I (1245)
14. Lyon II (1274)
15. Vienne (1311–1312)
16. Constance (1414–1418)
17. Basel, Ferrara, and Florence (1431–1445)
18. Lateran V (1512–1517)
19. Trent (1545–1563)
20. Vatican I (1869–1870)
21. Vatican II (1962–1965)

e. Answer *b* is correct.

21

The Bible is divinely inspired, which means

a. the sacred writers had visions and wrote down what they saw.

b. the sacred writers were given extraordinary literary skills by God, and this is why the Bible is so beautifully written.

c. God moved the sacred writers so that they wrote only and whatever he wanted them to write.

d. the Bible is the most inspiring book in the world.

e. none of the above.

a. Some of the sacred writers had visions, but most did not. Of the New Testament books, for instance, only one, Revelation, seems to have been the product of visions.

b. Some of the Bible is not at all beautifully written, and there is no disrespect in acknowledging this. For proof, try reading the two books of Chronicles. They read like lists of military statistics because that is what they chiefly are. Inspiration has nothing to do with literary skills or fineness of language.

c. This is what Vatican II said in the third chapter of *Dei Verbum*.

d. This is a different use of the term *inspiring*. In this sense it means "moving" (either emotionally or intellectually), and the ability to move the reader is independent of divine inspiration. Robert Frost's poems are not divinely inspired, but many people, no doubt, are lifted to emotional heights by reading them.

e. The correct answer is *c*.

22

Persons with same-sex attraction

    a. will go to hell unless they become heterosexuals first.

    b. are not responsible for their condition, so homosexual acts are not sinful for them.

    c. cannot be baptized.

    d. are under the same obligation of chastity as are unmarried heterosexuals.

    e. none of the above

a. Untrue, because the mere state of having same-sex attraction is not itself sinful.

b. Whether or not homosexual persons are responsible for their condition, they are morally responsible for any homosexual acts that they freely commit. Such acts always are gravely sinful (see Rom 1:26–27; 1 Cor 6:9–10; 1 Tim 1:9–10; Jude 7).

c. Any unbaptized person who is repentant of his sins and who believes what the Church teaches can be baptized. This includes people with same-sex attraction.

d. The obligation to chastity that homosexual persons live under is no greater than the one that unmarried heterosexual persons live under: no sexual relations outside marriage.

e. The answer directly above is right.

23

Who is the patron saint of altar servers?

   a. Bruno Bettelheim
   b. John Betjeman
   c. John Berchmans
   d. Loraine Boettner
   e. none of the above

a. Wrong. Bruno Bettelheim (1903–1990) was an Austrian-born American child psychologist.

b. Wrong again. John Betjeman (1906–1984) was named poet laureate of Britain in 1972 and was known for his insistent defense of Victorian architecture. When Betjeman studied at Oxford's Magdalen College, his tutor was C. S. Lewis. The two did not get along.

c. Yes, John Berchmans (1599–1621) is the answer. He was born in Diest, Belgium, died in Rome at age twenty-two, and was canonized in 1888. He was a Jesuit scholastic. There is a surprising American connection. Mary Wilson was a novice at the Academy of the Sacred Heart in Grand Coteau, Louisiana. In 1866, a year after Berchmans was beatified, he appeared to her. Seriously ill, Wilson had been unable to consume anything but liquids for forty days. At Berchmans' appearance she was immediately healed. This is the miracle that led to his canonization.

d. You should be ashamed of yourself. Go back and read chapter 2 of my book *Catholicism and Fundamentalism*. It is devoted to Loraine Boettner (1901–1990), a prominent anti-Catholic.

e. Answer *c* is right.

24

Statues

   a. really shouldn't be used by Catholics, according to Exodus 20:4–5, which warns against "graven images".

   b. have scriptural support in Exodus 25:18.

   c. are prayed to by Catholics because this is a pious practice sanctioned by the Church.

   d. are no longer recommended for use in churches, according to Vatican II.

   e. none of the above

a. The standard Fundamentalist complaint—and false. The admonition is against praying to those images or to the false gods they represent.

b. This is where the Lord instructs the Israelites to adorn the Ark of the Covenant with statues of angels. He seemed to have no problem with images, if they were used in the right way.

c. We don't pray to statues, but we pray to the saints represented by them and ask those saints to pray to God on our behalf. Similarly, we don't pray to a crucifix, but we pray to Christ, who is depicted on the crucifix. The crucifix helps us to keep our minds on our Lord's Passion and what he underwent to achieve our redemption. Similarly, images of saints—whether statues or paintings or mosaics—help us to keep in mind the virtues at which those saints excelled and to think about trying to develop those virtues in ourselves.

d. Vatican II said no such thing.

e. Answer *b* is correct.

25

Hosts used for Communion

    a. can be made of any kind of bread.

    b. have to be shaped as small disks.

    c. must be embossed with the letters *IHS*, which stand for "In His Service".

    d. may be made with additives such as sugar, salt, baking soda, or honey.

    e. none of the above

a. No. Valid matter for hosts is bread made with only wheaten flour and water.

b. There is no requirement regarding the shape of hosts.

c. There is no requirement that anything be embossed on hosts. The letters *IHS* do not stand for "In His Service" but for the name of Jesus, which are taken from the first three letters of his name in Greek (iota, eta, sigma) and recast in Latin letters.

d. Only wheaten flour mixed with plain water may be used to make hosts. If anything else is added to the mix in a notable quantity—meaning that you can notice that it's there—the resultant bread is invalid because, in common estimation, it no longer would be plain wheat bread. Thus, notable amounts of sugar, salt, baking soda, or honey—not to mention nuts or fruits or any grains other than wheat—will make the bread invalid matter for Mass. (See paragraph 48 of the 2004 instruction *Redemptionis Sacramentum* [*The Sacrament of Redemption*], which was issued by the Congregation for Divine Worship.) The only exception to this is leaven. Eastern Catholic Churches use leavened bread, while the Western or Roman Church uses unleavened bread. The presence or absence of leaven doesn't affect validity.

e. Answer *e* is correct.

26

If the Holy Roman Empire were still in existence, who would be the Holy Roman Emperor today?

   a. Pope Francis

   b. the president of Italy

   c. Archduke Karl of Austria

   d. the heir to the German throne

   e. none of the above

a. You should have guessed that the Holy Roman Emperor and the pope are not one and the same since some of the greatest squabbles in history have been between emperors and popes. There never was an emperor-pope.

b. Closer, but the modern state of Italy was created only in 1861, decades after the Holy Roman Empire came to an end in 1806, so how could Italy's president be the emperor?

c. Archduke Karl of Austria (Karl von Habsburg) is the head of the House of Habsburg and is the grandson of the last emperor of the Austro-Hungarian Empire (also called Karl of Austria [1887–1922]). The latter man's imperial ancestor Francis II was the last Holy Roman Emperor.

d. No, not the heir to the German throne. Think Austria, not Germany, as the venue of the Holy Roman Emperors.

e. The right answer is *c*.

27

Human souls

a. are composed of the lightest, most invisible material substance known to man.

b. are generated through the cocreative powers of their parents.

c. are emanations of the divine essence.

d. are recycled from people who have died.

e. none of the above

a. Souls are spirits, and spirits are not made of matter. All things are either spiritual or material or, in the case of man, both. But spirit is not matter, and matter is not spirit, no matter how light or invisible the matter may be. (Helium is light and invisible, but it is matter, not spirit.)

b. Correct. The soul is infused into the body at the instant of conception. Since conception occurs through the action of the parents, it is proper to call their action cocreative, in the sense of "cooperating with creation". The creation that they cooperate with is the instantaneous creation of the soul by God. Without their cooperation, he would not create the soul of their child.

c. This idea comes from Gnostic and Manichaean dualism and in modern times is taught by pantheists. It holds that human souls are generated through an outflowing of the divine substance. This is impossible, since such a teaching contradicts God's absolute simplicity. If souls could flow out of him, then he would be composed of parts (the souls and the rest of him), which is not possible. God, like all spirits, has no parts. He is a unity. Another problem was pointed out by Saint Augustine: "The soul is not a part of God, for, if it were, then it would be in every respect unchangeable and indestructible" (Epistle 166), but that is not true of any created thing.

d. This is reincarnation, which is incompatible with Christianity: "[I]t is appointed for men to die once, and after that comes judgment" (Heb 9:27). When you die, you are immediately judged, and you go to heaven, hell, or (temporarily) purgatory. You don't return to Earth in a new body.

e. Answer *b* is correct.

28

What sin *can't* your spouse commit, even in theory?

   a. final impenitence

   b. fornication

   c. assassination

   d. blasphemy against the Holy Spirit

   e. none of the above

a. Anyone can be impenitent on his deathbed, even your spouse.

b. Here's the right answer. Fornication is a sexual sin that can be committed only by two unmarried people. If one or both are married (but not to each other, of course), the sin is adultery. Thus, neither you nor your spouse is capable of committing fornication. G. K. Chesterton's fictional detective-priest, Father Brown, said that any man is capable of committing any crime. That may be true for crimes, but it isn't quite true for sins.

c. You might think your spouse is incapable of assassination, but are you really sure?

d. It is possible for anyone to blaspheme against the Holy Spirit.

e. Answer *b* is correct.

29

The Old Testament

a. has more books in the Protestant version of the Bible because Protestants emphasize the Old Testament over the New Testament.

b. has more books in the Catholic version of the Bible because the Protestant Reformers threw out seven books at the Council of Trent.

c. was used by the early Christians in its Greek translation, known as the Septuagint.

d. no longer has authority over Christians but still has authority over Jews.

e. none of the above

a. No. It's the Catholic Old Testament, not the Protestant, that has seven additional books.

b. Hmmm. Better, but the Council of Trent was a Catholic council, not a Protestant council.

c. This is it!

d. No. Both Testaments are authoritative for Christians.

e. You might have chosen this answer if you hadn't heard of the Septuagint, but it's the wrong answer. See *c*.

30

Baptism may be administered by

    a. a priest or bishop only.

    b. a bishop, priest, or deacon only.

    c. any baptized Catholic only.

    d. unbaptized persons.

    e. none of the above.

a. This must be wrong, since even you can baptize.

b. Still wrong, since you probably aren't a bishop, priest, or deacon.

c. Closer yet, but still not right.

d. Yes, anyone, even a non-Christian, can baptize. Baptism may be administered by any person, provided that he intends to do what the Church does—even if he doesn't fully understand what the Church does in baptism—and uses the right words ("I baptize you in the name of the Father, and of the Son, and of the Holy Spirit") and actions (pouring or sprinkling water on the recipient's head or immersing the recipient in water). This means that a valid baptism can be administered by a Jew, a Muslim, a Hindu, an agnostic, or even an atheist. This is testimony not to Christ's capriciousness in establishing baptism but to how important baptism is. Our Lord wanted to make baptism as easily available as possible because this sacrament is the entrance to the life of grace.

e. Many quiz takers, knowing that laymen can baptize, think *c* is a trick answer because it excludes baptism by non-Catholic Christians. Then they wrongly conclude this is the right answer. The correct answer, however, is *d*.

3 1

To be elected pope, a man must at least be

    a. a cardinal who attends the papal conclave and is less than eighty years of age.

    b. baptized.

    c. over fifty years of age.

    d. fluent in Latin

    e. none of the above.

a. Although for centuries all popes have been selected from the ranks of the cardinals, there is no rule that a pope must be selected from their ranks.

b. Correct. The candidate must be a baptized Catholic; he can even be a married layman.

c. Nope. There is no age requirement. Benedict IX (1012–1056) was only twenty when he was elected pope, and John XII (930/937–964) was somewhere between eighteen and twenty-five, the year of his birth not being known with certitude. Of course, there is no likelihood that such a young person could be elected pope nowadays, but this does illustrate that there is no minimum age. There also is no maximum age. The oldest pope, at the time of his election, was Clement X, who was elected at age seventy-nine in 1670. Alexander VIII was only a few months younger when he was elected in 1689. Pope Francis, at his election, was the ninth-oldest man to be elected.

d. Fluency in Latin is a fine thing, but it is not a requirement for holding papal office.

e. The minimalistic answer *b* is correct.

32

Apparitions of Mary

    a. are only pious illusions, but the Church does not forbid belief in them.

    b. must be believed, if they are authentic, since any authentic revelation must be believed.

    c. bind in conscience, if they are authentic, only the recipients of the apparitions.

    d. are infallibly determined to have occurred if they are approved by the Church.

    e. none of the above

a. Some apparitions are illusions or just plain bogus, but some are real.

b. You must believe in general revelation but are free to reject any private revelation or apparition, even one approved by a Church authority, such as a bishop or even a pope. General revelation ceased with the death of the last apostle (about A.D. 100) and is found in Scripture and Sacred Tradition. Any later revelation is called private revelation, no matter how many people may be informed of it.

c. Only the recipient of a private apparition is bound in conscience to follow it, if he thinks it is real. Anyone else is free to ignore a private apparition, even those who are convinced that a particular private apparition actually occurred. (This is not to say that you are free to ignore whatever true teachings are repeated through an apparition. Truth is truth, no matter where it appears.)

d. Even approved apparitions are not guaranteed by the Church to have occurred. Approval means only that nothing that purportedly has been taught via an apparition is contrary to the faith or to good morals.

e. The rather minimalistic *c* is correct.

33

In the Mass

a. Jesus is symbolized by the bread and the wine from the moment of Consecration onward.

b. Jesus is spiritually present when the community gathers in prayer under the leadership of the priest and ceases to be spiritually present when the priest leaves the sanctuary.

c. Jesus is physically present along with the bread and the wine once the Consecration has occurred.

d. Jesus is present, and the bread and the wine are not present, after the Consecration.

e. none of the above

a. Jesus is not symbolized by the bread and the wine—they actually become him.

b. Jesus is more than just spiritually present during Mass, and he remains present in the consecrated elements until they cease to look like bread and wine. The priest's presence in the sanctuary is irrelevant (except at the Consecration, of course).

c. Although physically present, Jesus is not present along with the bread and the wine. They cease to be present in their essences after the Consecration; only their appearances (technical term: accidents) remain. The idea that Christ's Body and Blood exist alongside the bread and the wine is the heresy of consubstantiation.

d. Correct, because the bread and the wine cease to be present in their essence or substance after the Consecration. Only Jesus is present.

e. Wrong, because *d* is correct.

34

The doctrine of the Trinity means

    a. there is one God who manifests himself in the three distinct roles of the Father, the Son, and the Holy Spirit.

    b. that since the Resurrection there have been four Persons in the Trinity: the Father, the Son, the Holy Spirit, and Jesus Christ the God-Man.

    c. that in the Godhead there is only one divine Person, and he takes on different aspects according to his actions as Creator, Redeemer, or Sanctifier.

    d. there are three gods who work so closely together that it is proper to call them one God.

    e. none of the above.

a. This is the heresy of Modalism, which says there is but one Person in the Godhead and that Person, so to speak, wears different "masks" according to his different roles as Father, Son, or Holy Spirit. Modalism, also known as Sabellianism, flourished in the third and fourth centuries.

b. This is a nonsense answer. The very word *Trinity* comes from the Latin prefix meaning "three" (*tri*), so you should see right away that a Trinity could not be composed of four Persons.

c. Wrong, because this is just a rephrasing, in gender-neutral language, of *a*.

d. Christians are monotheists and believe in one God, not three. No matter how closely together three gods work, they would remain three gods, not one.

e. Correct, because all the other possible answers are wrong.

35

An archbishop

    a. is always an older bishop and, by canon law, must be at least fifty-five years of age.

    b. has jurisdiction over all the bishops within his metropolitan area and may overrule their decisions.

    c. assists the pope by voting on prospective cardinals.

    d. is a regular bishop who has been given the honorary title of archbishop by leading bishops in his national bishops' conference.

    e. none of the above

a. Canon law provides no age requirement for the office of archbishop.

b. Diocesan bishops (ordinaries), as distinguished from auxiliary bishops, have only the pope as their boss, although, for ceremonial purposes, archbishops take the lead over bishops within their metropolitan areas.

c. Cardinals are not selected by voting. Popes choose them directly.

d. A man becomes an archbishop by being named by the pope to an archiepiscopal see. Such sees normally are in larger cities or have had some historical importance.

e. Correct, because all the other possible answers are wrong.

36

The vessel that holds water at the door to Catholic churches may be called any of these *except*

    a. a stoup.

    b. a font.

    c. a holy water holder.

    d. a mandamus bowl.

    e. none of the above.

a. It seems people either think of this word first or never heard of the word at all.

b. *Font* is a synonym and perhaps in more common use today.

c. While in no way a regular title, this phrase accurately describes the apparatus, so this isn't the right answer either.

d. Ah, here we are. *Mandamus* sounds as though it might have something to do with the Maundy Thursday foot-washing ceremony, but not so. The word actually means a writ issued by a superior court, generally to an inferior court, ordering the performance of a certain act.

e. The right answer is *d*.

37

Veneration of images of saints

    a. is prohibited in the Eastern Catholic Churches.

    b. was promoted by the eighth-century group known as the Iconoclasts.

    c. is termed "relative *dulia*", in contrast to "absolute *dulia*", which is the veneration given to the saints themselves.

    d. is a lesser form of veneration called *hyperdulia*.

    e. none of the above

a. Quite the contrary, Eastern Catholic Churches make wide use of images—chiefly mosaics and paintings—and veneration of the images is encouraged.

b. The Iconoclasts engaged in iconoclasm, the deliberate destruction of religious images. The most famous outbreak of iconoclasm occurred from 730 to 787. A rogue council, convened by a Byzantine emperor in 754, formalized opposition to the use of images, even though Pope Gregory III had convoked, in 730, a synod that condemned iconoclasm as heretical. An ecumenical council, Second Nicaea (787), formally approved the use of images.

c. True, veneration given to images is one step removed from veneration given to those represented by the images. We have a parallel of this in our homes: we put in a place of honor photographs of our parents or other relatives; we honor the photographs only because we honor those depicted in them.

d. Given her dignity as the Mother of God and her preservation from sin, the Virgin Mary is entitled to a special level of veneration. This is far less than the adoration due to God, but it is higher than the veneration given to other saints and to angels. The latter veneration is called *dulia* (which means "veneration"), and the form rendered to Mary is called *hyperdulia*. Thus, *hyperdulia* is a higher, not a lower, form of veneration.

e. Answer *c* is correct.

38

How many popes have been of Jewish descent?

   a. only one, Peter

   b. two, Peter and his immediate successor, Linus

   c. Only three of the first four popes; after the Jewish Council of Jamnia (ca. A.D. 80), which promulgated the finalized Jewish canon of the Bible, no further popes of Jewish descent were elected.

   d. more than three

   e. none of the above

a. Yes, Peter was of Jewish descent, but he wasn't the only pope who was.

b. Sorry, there were more than two.

c. There is not much historical evidence that Jewish leaders held a council at Jamnia. That such a council occurred was a conclusion drawn in 1871 by Heinrich Graetz, a Jewish historian born in what is now Poland. Jamnia, also known as Yavne, is the place where the Sanhedrin relocated after the Temple was destroyed by the Romans in A.D. 70. Even if a council was held at Jamnia, it isn't true that no further popes of Jewish descent reigned after that time.

d. No one knows how many popes have been of Jewish descent, but in the eleventh and twelfth centuries there were three: Gregory VI, Gregory VII, and Anacletus II. Add Peter to their number, and you get more than three, so this is the right answer.

e. Look right above.

39

When did seminary training for priests become common?

a. at the beginning of Church history, with our Lord's teaching in the Temple

b. after the promulgation of Pope Pius X's encyclical *Educationis Seminarii*

c. after the Council of Trent

d. at an unknown early date, because diocesan seminaries were in regular use by the time of Augustine

e. none of the above

a. Sorry, but you're about fifteen hundred years off.

b. There never has been an encyclical titled *Educationis Seminarii*.

c. Correct. The Council of Trent attempted to regularize priestly training—a much-needed reform of the Church.

d. Prior to Trent, priests were trained in an apprentice system: young men lived and worked with priests until they learned what to do, and then they were ordained—great if your teacher was Augustine, but disastrous if your teacher was himself ignorant of the faith.

e. The right answer is *c*.

40

The four cardinal virtues are

    a. prudence, piety, faithfulness, and peaceableness.
    b. temperance, holiness, charity, and wisdom.
    c. courage, fortitude, bravery, and fearlessness.
    d. fortitude, temperance, abstinence, and hope.
    e. none of the above.

a. You're starting out right, with prudence, but then you go off the rails.

b. Temperance is another cardinal virtue, but the others are not.

c. These four words are virtually synonymous; the one usually listed among the cardinal virtues is fortitude.

d. The first two are right. The last two, while admirable, are not cardinal virtues.

e. The four cardinal virtues are prudence, temperance, fortitude, and justice.

41

Original sin is transmitted by

    a. imitation.

    b. bad example.

    c. bad arguments.

    d. the matrilineal line of Eve.

    e. none of the above.

a. The Council of Trent rejected this idea, saying that original sin is inherited by Adam's posterity through descent, not through imitation. It is transmitted in the same way as human nature, through the natural act of generation. All of us suffer the effects of original sin from the first moment of our existence.

b. This was a notion most famously associated with Pelagius, a British monk who died in 418. He taught that moral perfection is attainable through one's own will and that grace is not necessary to achieve this perfection. Sin, he said, is transmitted by bad examples (which are countless) and so in theory can be avoided entirely. The great opponent of Pelagianism, the heresy named after Pelagius, was Saint Augustine (354–430).

c. By the time anyone has heard a bad argument, he already has been living with the effects of original sin (since his conception), so this can't be the right answer.

d. It is Adam who gets the blame for original sin, and so it is from him, not Eve, that it is transmitted to us, even though she was complicit in the sin.

e. None of the above answers is correct, so this one is.

42

The Consecration of the Eucharist

   a. can be performed by a Catholic priest or by a priest of an Eastern Orthodox Church.

   b. can be performed by a Catholic priest only if he celebrates Mass with at least two witnesses.

   c. can be performed by Catholic priests and Anglican priests so long as they have the proper intention and pronounce the correct words of Consecration.

   d. can be performed by deacons and specially commissioned laypersons in emergency situations.

   e. none of the above

a. Correct, because the Eastern Orthodox Churches have the seven sacraments and therefore a real priesthood. It takes a real priest to confect the Real Presence.

b. Wrong, because a priest may celebrate Mass by himself. The validity of the Mass does not depend on the presence of witnesses. Perhaps you are confusing here the validity of a marriage, which normally requires two witnesses.

c. Wrong, because Anglican orders are not valid. Out of courtesy we call Anglican ministers "Father", but Pope Leo XIII definitely determined in 1896 that Anglican orders long ago became defective. In *Apostolicae Curae* he said that Anglican ordinations are "absolutely null and utterly void". The logical conclusion is that Anglican priests are, technically, Christian laymen. Since they aren't actually priests—despite the courtesy title—their having the proper intention and their pronouncing the correct words of Consecration are immaterial.

d. Wrong, because deacons, while having orders, do not have priestly orders, and laypeople have no orders at all. You need priestly orders to consecrate the Eucharist.

e. Wrong, because *a* is correct.

43

A deacon is

a. a priest who does not have permission to celebrate Mass until after his wife dies.

b. a layman who may distribute Communion, marry people, baptize babies, and wear vestments.

c. a man who has received the first level of holy orders and is neither a priest nor a layman.

d. forbidden to hear confessions and give absolution except in emergency situations and in the absence of a priest.

e. none of the above.

a. A deacon is not a married priest. Married priests are called, well, married priests, and they are common in some of the Eastern Churches. (There are even a few in the Western Church.) When a deacon's wife dies, he remains a deacon; he does not suddenly acquire priestly powers at her death.

b. Although deacons may do all these things, they are not laymen. They are ordained to the first level of holy orders, but they are not priests.

c. Correct, because a deacon is no longer a layman and is not a priest.

d. A deacon never can give sacramental absolution, for the simple reason that he is not a priest and doesn't have the power to grant sacramental absolution.

e. Answer *c* is correct.

44

God knows

    a. all things in the past, the present, and the future.

    b. all things in the past and the present, but he knows things in the future only after they have occurred.

    c. all things in the present only.

    d. all present and future things, but God intentionally forgets things that are in the past because what's done is done.

    e. none of the above.

a. This is the right answer because God knows everything, and "everything" is made up of things that are past, things that are present, and things that are yet to occur.

b. This makes no sense. If God knows future things only after they have occurred, then he knows them only once they have become past things, which means he does not know future things at all.

c. If this were true, God would not know about things in the past—but we would know about some past things, which would make us more knowledgeable than God, at least concerning those things.

d. It's true that what's done is done, but that doesn't mean God throws his knowledge of such things down the memory hole.

e. The obvious answer, *a*, is the right answer.

45

In cases of necessity, which of the following is acceptable matter for baptism?

a. beer
b. lite beer, but not other kinds of beer
c. blood (hence "baptism of blood")
d. sea water
e. none of the above

a. No, because the liquid used must be considered to be water in common parlance. Scripture teaches that baptism is performed with water, "born of water" (Jn 3:5; see also Acts 8:36; 10:47; Eph 5:26; Heb 10:22). The oldest liturgical document we have, the *Didache* (*Teaching of the Twelve Apostles*, written around the end of the first century), provides: "Baptize in the name of the Father and of the Son and of the Holy Spirit in living [flowing] water. If you have no living water, then baptize in another water. If you cannot do it in cold, do it in warm. If you have neither [in sufficient quantity], then pour water on the head three times, in the name of the Father, and of the Son, and of the Holy Spirit."

b. Taking out the calories doesn't help.

c. "Baptism of blood" refers to martyrdom; sacramental baptism is water baptism and requires water.

d. Yes, sea water works, since it is commonly accounted as water, even if not potable.

e. The correct answer is *d*.

46

Which of the following is a defined Catholic dogma?

a. limbo
b. purgatory
c. both limbo and purgatory
d. priestly celibacy
e. none of the above

a. Limbo is not a defined dogma. It is a theological speculation, and good Catholics may believe or not believe in it, as the arguments move them. Limbo remains "a possible theological hypothesis", according to *The Hope of Salvation for Infants Who Die without Being Baptized*, a document released by the International Theological Commission in 2007. Pope Benedict XVI authorized the document's publication. Of course, if the Church were to define formally the existence or nonexistence of limbo, everyone would be obliged in conscience to fall in line.

b. Yes, purgatory is an official dogma of the Church. Even though it is not much talked about today, Catholics still must believe in it. It is not an optional belief.

c. Wrong, because only purgatory is a defined dogma.

d. Priestly celibacy is a custom or discipline, not a dogma.

e. Answer *b* is correct.

47

What is the proper way to interpret the Bible, particularly its disputed or controversial passages?

   a. literally
   b. figuratively
   c. slowly
   d. discursively
   e. none of the above

a. Not just literally, which is what Protestant Fundamentalists tend to argue. Although much of the Bible should be interpreted literally, some parts (the poetry in the Song of Solomon, for example) should be read figuratively.

b. Not just figuratively, since most of the Bible should be read literally.

c. It may be good to read the Bible slowly, to make sure the words sink in, but slowness is not a method of interpretation.

d. An interpretation may be explained discursively, but discursiveness is not itself a method of interpretation.

e. Each of the other four answers includes or implies something false (such as that the Bible should be interpreted *only* literally or *only* figuratively). Thus "none of the above" is correct.

48

What is the dogma of the Immaculate Conception?

a. Mary conceived Jesus immaculately in her womb, without the aid of a human father.

b. Mary conceived Jesus immaculately in her womb, and he remained without sin.

c. Mary was conceived immaculately in her mother's womb, without the aid of a human father.

d. Mary was conceived immaculately in her mother's womb and was preserved from sin.

e. none of the above

a. This defines not the Immaculate Conception but the Virgin Birth of Jesus (that is, the birth of Jesus from a Virgin).

b. It is true that Jesus remained without sin and was conceived immaculately, but the dogma of the Immaculate Conception concerns Mary's conception, not Jesus'.

c. No, because Mary had a human father. It is believed that her mother's name was Anne and her father's Joachim.

d. Correct, because the main consequence of the Immaculate Conception is that Mary was able to live a sinless life. (She could have sinned, had she so chosen, but she chose not to; Adam and Eve could have chosen not to sin, but they chose to sin.)

e. Answer *d* is correct.

49

To guarantee your salvation, you must

    a. keep at least a majority of the Ten Commandments.

    b. wear a scapular daily.

    c. die in the state of sanctifying grace, even if you committed a mortal sin the day before.

    d. go to confession at least monthly.

    e. none of the above

a. If you keep only a majority of the Ten Commandments, that means you are not keeping some of them. Nowhere did Christ suggest that salvation can be obtained for doing only a halfway job.

b. There is no requirement to wear a scapular, and wearing a scapular is no guarantee of heaven.

c. This is the correct answer: to get to heaven, you must die with sanctifying grace in your soul. If you die without accepting that grace, you go to hell. If you die in the state of sanctifying grace with some attachment to sin, you go to purgatory first, to rid yourself of that attachment. After that, you head for heaven.

d. Frequent confession is meritorious. The sacrament of confession returns sanctifying grace to the soul. It is that grace that is needed for salvation, not the participation in the sacrament.

e. Answer *c* is correct.

50

Papal infallibility means

    a. the pope is preserved by the Holy Spirit from committing mortal sins.

    b. anything the pope teaches is guaranteed by the Holy Spirit to be true.

    c. the pope's teachings must be assented to because he is under the guidance of the Holy Spirit and thus speaks for the Holy Spirit, who cannot err.

    d. the pope is incapable of teaching erroneously on matters of faith and morals when he defines publicly and officially a doctrine for all Christians, not just Catholics, to hold.

    e. none of the above.

a. This is the notion of impeccability—the inability to sin. Only Jesus was impeccable. It has nothing to do with infallibility, which means the inability to err.

b. The pope's infallibility is guaranteed only when he speaks officially on matters of faith and morals. If he tells you who will win the next World Series, keep your betting money in your pocket.

c. It is true that the pope's teaching (even his noninfallible teaching) must be given due assent, but this isn't what the doctrine of infallibility means.

d. Correct, as defined formally at Vatican I (1870).

e. Answer *d* is correct.

51

Contraception is

a. permissible only for married couples with the permission of their parish priest and under extenuating circumstances.

b. never permissible, no matter what the circumstances.

c. permissible if the husband and wife, after honest prayer, conclude that it is right for them and do not use it selfishly.

d. permissible only if the wife's health would otherwise be in danger or if the husband is unable to support a large family.

e. none of the above.

a. Wrong, because a priest cannot give anyone permission to engage in any sinful act.

b. Correct, as explained in Pope Paul VI's 1968 encyclical *Humanae Vitae*. It is immaterial that most Catholics don't practice what the Church always has preached. Truth is not determined by majority vote.

c. This is a cop-out. Contraception is always immoral and does not become moral just because some couples agree not to use it "selfishly". Do bank heists become moral if the thieves agree to distribute the proceeds not to themselves but to the poor?

d. A good motive cannot make an evil act good. If there is a problem with the wife's health or the family's pocketbook, the couple should consider natural family planning (which is not the same as the rhythm method); it can be used morally because it does not subvert the procreative potential of the conjugal act.

e. Wrong, because *b* is correct.

52

A nun

    a. is neither a layperson nor a cleric.

    b. is a cleric and no longer a layperson.

    c. may be installed as a chaplain of a hospital.

    d. is the female equivalent of a deacon.

    e. none of the above

a. Wrong, because sisters (women religious), like brothers (men religious), are laypeople. They are not ordained—they take vows, which is different.

b. Nuns are not ordained, and only the ordained are clerics. There are three grades of clerics: deacons, priests, and bishops.

c. Wrong, even though in some places sisters are termed chaplains. According to canon law (canon 564), chaplains, properly speaking, are priests. It isn't correct to call someone a chaplain merely because he provides some sort of spiritual counseling.

d. This is wrong because deacons are ordained and nuns are not.

e. Correct, because all the other possible answers are wrong.

53

Which of these is an accurate definition of a heresy?

a. Jansenism, named after Cornelius Jansen (1585–1638), taught that Christ died for all and that therefore everyone is predestined to be saved.

b. Monophysitism (also called Eutychianism) taught that there was only one (*mono*) permissible way to receive Holy Communion, and that was in the form of bread alone.

c. Adoptionism taught that Jesus was the Father's adopted Son.

d. Brunoism, named after Giordano Bruno (1548–1600), the Italian friar, philosopher, and astrologer who was burned at the stake in Rome's Campo de' Fiori, held that the Bible could be understood sufficiently through science, without need for a Magisterium.

e. none of the above

a. Jansenists held that Christ died only for the elect and that the sign of God's election is the ability to live a life of extreme austerity and moral uprightness. The result of this thinking often was severe scrupulosity, the error of seeing sin where there is no sin.

b. Monophysitism comes from the Greek term for "one nature". This heresy, which arose in the fifth century, claimed that Christ had a single nature that somehow combined divine and human elements. This contradicts the Catholic doctrine that Christ has two complete and distinct natures.

c. Correct. Adoptionism was a second-century heresy that held that Jesus became the Son of God at his baptism, his Resurrection, or his Ascension (theories differed). This implied that he did not start out as God and therefore was only a creature, even if the most exalted. Adoptionism was condemned at the First Council of Nicaea in 325.

d. It is true that Bruno was a heretic, but there is no heresy named after him.

e. Answer *c* is correct.

54

The sacrament of confession

   a. almost always must be received before receiving Communion by anyone guilty of a mortal sin since his last confession.

   b. is not necessary because you can privately and sincerely confess your sins to God.

   c. must be received by all Catholic adults at least once a year (one of the six precepts of the Church)

   d. is useless if you have committed one of the four sins that cry to heaven for vengeance—murder (Gen 4:10), sodomy (Gen 18:20–21), oppression of the poor (Ex 2:23), and defrauding workers of just wages (Jas 5:4)—because those sins can't be forgiven.

   e. none of the above

a. Correct. If you have committed a mortal sin, you may not receive Communion until after you have gone to sacramental confession "unless there is a grave reason and no opportunity to confess" (*Code of Canon Law*, 916).

b. No, because this would imply that Jesus set up a superfluous sacrament (confession), and he never did anything superfluously. See John 20:21–23: "Jesus said to them again, 'Peace be with you. As the Father has sent me, even so I send you.' And when he had said this, he breathed on them, and said to them, 'Receive the Holy Spirit. If you forgive the sins of any, they are forgiven; if you retain the sins of any, they are retained.'"

c. This is not one of the six precepts of the Church, for the simple reason that you need to go to confession only if you commit a mortal sin, though it is good to go frequently even if you commit only venial sins. (You might be thinking of the precept to receive Communion once a year, during the Easter season.)

d. There is no sin, no matter how grave, that can't be forgiven in confession, so long as the sinner truly is repentant.

e. Answer *a* is correct.

55

At the Crucifixion

    a. Jesus' human nature died on the cross.

    b. only the human person of Jesus, not the divine Person of Jesus, died on the cross.

    c. God died on the cross.

    d. Jesus' human and divine natures both died on the cross, but the universe was kept going by the Father and the Holy Spirit until Jesus' Resurrection.

    e. none of the above

a. Wrong, because natures aren't put to death—persons are. When you die, it is not your human nature that dies but you as a distinct person.

b. There is no human person in Jesus. There is only one Person, the divine, who already (by definition) had a divine nature and who took on a human nature. Nestorianism was a fourth- and fifth-century heresy that taught that in Christ there were two distinct persons, one human and one divine. A consequence of this teaching was the rejection of the term *Theotokos* ("God-bearer") for the Virgin Mary, since she supposedly gave birth only to a human person, not to a divine Person.

c. Correct, because the Person who died on the cross was a divine Person, commonly called the Son of God. Since that Person is God, it is proper to say that God died on the cross, even though that sounds odd and may make some unthinking people conclude that it means that God ceased to exist, which, of course, was not the case. (If you were sure this answer could not be right, don't fret—you're in good company. Most people miss this question because the correct answer just doesn't sound right.)

d. Wrong, first, because natures don't die, persons do, and second, because the answer suggests that Jesus couldn't keep the universe going, as though he ceased to be God between the time of his death and his Resurrection.

e. Answer *c* is correct.

56

Purgatory is

a. a state of natural happiness where souls of unbaptized
   infants and morally good non-Christians will wait until
   they are judged on the Last Day.

b. a state of mild punishment for people who were not bad
   enough to go to hell and who were not good enough to
   go to heaven.

c. a state of purification for people who die in the state of
   grace but without complete love for God.

d. a temporary state where sincere people who do not die in
   the state of grace get a second chance to do good and thus
   avoid going to hell.

e. none of the above.

a. What is described is almost (not quite) the definition of *limbo*—not quite because limbo is posited to be a permanent state of natural happiness, not one that will end on the Last Day. In any case, limbo is not a defined teaching of the Church; it is a theological speculation, and one is free to believe or not believe in it.

b. Wrong, first, because the answer suggests that purgatory is a permanent abode for some people (in fact, it will be emptied or even cease to exist at the end of the world when the last person leaves it for heaven); second, because the answer suggests that purgatory is for people who are not good enough to go to heaven. In fact, it is precisely for people who are good enough to go to heaven—but not quite yet; everyone who goes to purgatory will go to heaven.

c. Correct, because purgatory is a state in which the last vestiges of self-love are removed, so we might enter heaven according to Revelation 21:27, which says that "nothing unclean shall enter it."

d. No. You go around only once in life ("[I]t is appointed for men to die once, and after that comes judgment" [Heb 9:27]). Your soul is judged immediately after your death, and your fate is sealed then.

e. The correct answer is *c*.

57

Priests

    a. were first ordained by Jesus when he told the apostles, "Do this in remembrance of me."

    b. were first ordained by Paul on his visit to Corinth.

    c. first appeared late in the second century, perhaps in Asia Minor. Before that, local churches were led by presbyters.

    d. first appeared in the 1200s. Previously, parishes operated on the congregational system, with members choosing a presiding minister from among their own number. Not until the High Middle Ages was this formalized into an ordained priesthood, with the priest chosen not by the congregation but by the bishop.

    e. none of the above

a. Yes. See Luke 22:19, which is part of the account of the Last Supper: "And he took bread, and when he had given thanks he broke it and gave it to them, saying, 'This is my body which is given for you. Do this in remembrance of me.'" Here Christ establishes the sacrament of the Eucharist. He instructs his apostles to do in their turn what he is doing in his: offer the sacrifice of his Body. One who offers a sacrifice is a priest, and Christ is the High Priest of the New Covenant.

b. Not possible, since the first answer is correct. Paul visited Corinth roughly twenty years after the Last Supper occurred.

c. Even less possible. Think about it: if priests didn't appear until late in the first century, why do they appear in the New Testament, such as in Paul's epistles? The word *presbyter* is used in the New Testament chiefly to distinguish the New Testament priesthood from the still-existing Jewish priesthood, but *presbyter* and *priest* amount to the same thing.

d. Please think of enrolling in a basic Church history course.

e. You should have had no trouble seeing that *a* is correct.

58

An annulment is

   a. the canon law equivalent of a divorce under civil law.

   b. a Church-authorized dissolution of a marriage that has failed through the infidelity of one of the spouses.

   c. a declaration that no valid sacramental marriage existed in the first place, even if there are children born during the relationship.

   d. a declaration that children born in a failed marriage are not illegitimate.

   e. none of the above.

a. There is no canon law equivalent of civil divorce because sacramental marriages can't be ended by divorce. Once married, always married—until "death do you part."

b. A sacramental marriage, once made, is not undone even if one of the spouses becomes unfaithful. Only death ends a sacramental marriage.

c. Correct, because the existence of children from the relationship is not a bar to being granted a decree of nullity.

d. An annulment (more properly, a decree of nullity) is a marriage tribunal's decision that no valid sacramental marriage existed in the first place. It is not a decision about the legitimacy or illegitimacy of children. (Church law holds that children born in putative marriages that are later annulled are to be considered legitimate.)

e. Wrong, because *c* is correct.

59

Parish pastoral councils

a. were set up by Vatican II to oversee the work of parish priests.

b. prevail against the opinions of pastors if at least two-thirds of the council members agree on an issue.

c. advise the pastor but have no authority over him.

d. were instituted by Vatican II because the Church is now a democracy, not a monarchy.

e. none of the above

a. Wrong, for two reasons: Vatican II did not set up parish councils (they predate the council), and parish councils are not above parish priests but work under the supervision and oversight of parish priests, particularly pastors.

b. This is just a supermajority variation of *a* and thus is a wrong answer.

c. Correct, because parish pastoral councils are under the pastor, who, under canon law, is subject in his running of the parish only to his bishop and to the Vatican.

d. Wrong, because Vatican II did not institute them and because the Church remains a monarchy, not a democracy, in that she mirrors the organization of heaven, which is a monarchy with Christ as the King.

e. Answer *c* is correct.

60

Mortal sin

   a. is nowhere mentioned in Scripture.

   b. is a theological construct from the Church of the Middle Ages, and since Vatican II we recognize that there are only two kinds of sins, venial and serious.

   c. is the same as serious sin; only the words are different.

   d. makes it impossible for you ever to get to heaven, no matter what you do.

   e. none of the above

a. Mortal sin is mentioned in 1 John 5:17: "All wrongdoing is sin, but there is sin which is not deadly", which implies that some sin is deadly.

b. Serious sin is exactly the same as mortal sin. Only the words differ.

c. Correct; see *b*.

d. No, you can go to heaven if you die after repenting of a mortal sin.

e. Answer *c* is correct.

61

Apologetics means

    a. never having to say you're sorry.

    b. the art of apologizing for being a Catholic.

    c. a course that seminarians used to have to take but are now exempted from by canon law.

    d. giving reasoned explanations and defenses for the faith.

    e. none of the above.

a. Maybe you saw the movie *Love Story* too many times.

b. This betrays a penchant for using the colloquial meaning of a word when trying to decide on the word's definition. Apologetics has nothing to do with saying "I'm sorry."

c. Once upon a time, nearly every seminary had courses in apologetics. Then, for some decades, those courses just about disappeared from the scene. In recent years some seminaries have been bringing them back. In any case, seminarians are not exempted from taking such courses by canon law.

d. Correct. Need one say more?

e. Back up one answer.

62

A Mass is invalid

   a. if "Kumbaya" is sung.

   b. if the priest omits the opening Sign of the Cross and the Nicene Creed.

   c. if the priest celebrates Mass while he is in the state of mortal sin.

   d. if the priest ad-libs any part of the canon.

   e. none of the above

a. For a while in the sixties we nearly thought so, but no.

b. It is illicit for a priest to omit the opening Sign of the Cross or, when specified by the rubrics, the Creed, but such omissions do not make the Mass invalid.

c. Wrong, because the efficacy of any sacrament does not depend on the holiness of the minister. If so, we could never tell if absolution "took" in the confessional or if a Mass was validly celebrated, since we can't see inside the priest's soul. Sacraments work through their own power, given by Christ, not through the virtuousness of the priest.

d. Still wrong, but close. If a priest ad-libs the words of consecration, he likely will end up with an invalid Mass. If he ad-libs other parts of the canon, he acts illicitly and perhaps sinfully, but the Mass does not become invalid.

e. Correct, because all the other possible answers are wrong.

63

Which of these is not one of the five proofs for the existence of God as given by Saint Thomas Aquinas?

   a. the argument of an unmoved mover

   b. the argument of Pascal's wager

   c. the argument of a first cause

   d. the argument from contingency

   e. none of the above

a. The argument of an unmoved mover states that everything that changes (not just in location but in any other sense) must have something that changes it. The thing that changes it must itself have something that changes *it*. We can keep going backward, but not infinitely. There must be an original changer (or unmoved mover) that is not changed or moved itself, and that is God.

b. Pascal's wager—that it is more reasonable to presume God's existence and to act as though he exists than to presume his nonexistence and be unpleasantly surprised in the afterlife— was made by, of course, Blaise Pascal (1623–1662), who lived long after Thomas Aquinas (1225–1274).

c. The argument of a first cause states that everything is caused by something else. There can't be an infinite line of causes, so there must be a first cause, which is God. This is similar to the argument of an unmoved mover.

d. The argument from contingency says that things that now exist need not have existed and thus are contingent— dependent for their existence on something else. If *everything* were contingent, there would have been a time when nothing at all existed. In that state, there would be no way for anything to come into existence. Thus, there must be something that is not contingent (that is, something that *must* exist), and that something is God.

e. The correct answer is *b*.

64

Which of these sacraments does *not* forgive mortal sins?

   a. anointing of the sick
   b. Eucharist
   c. baptism
   d. extreme unction
   e. none of the above

a. The anointing of the sick removes sin, confers grace, and can even strengthen bodily.

b. This is the correct answer. During the Mass, venial sins can be forgiven either during the penitential rite or through the reception of Holy Communion, but mortals sins cannot be forgiven in those ways.

c. Baptism wipes out all sins, including original sin and actual sins (that is, sins we commit through our own acts after we reach the age of reason, traditionally put at around seven years of age).

d. Extreme unction is another name for anointing of the sick.

e. Answer *b* is correct.

65

Which of these is a proper chronological listing of ecumenical councils?

   a. Nicaea, Ephesus, First Lateran, Second Constantinople
   b. Chalcedon, Ephesus, Trent, Vatican I
   c. Third Nicaea, Second Lateran, Trent, Vatican II
   d. Fourth Constantinople, Chalcedon, First Lyon, Constance
   e. none of the above

a. No: Nicaea (325), Ephesus (431), First Lateran (1123), Second Constantinople (553).

b. No: Chalcedon (451), Ephesus (431), Trent (1545–1563), Vatican I (1869–1870).

c. No, because there was no Third Nicaea.

d. No: Fourth Constantinople (869–870), Chalcedon (451), First Lyon (1245), Constance (1414–1418).

e. None of the above answers is correct, so this one is.

66

The Church founded by Christ

    a. came to be the Catholic Church after Christianity was legalized by the Roman emperor Constantine.

    b. is called "Catholic", which means "universal", because she is found in every country in the world.

    c. began at Christ's Ascension and will continue until the end of the world.

    d. is a perfect society.

    e. none of the above

a. The Church started out as the Catholic Church, though that title was not used immediately. The first recorded use is from A.D. 107, in the *Letter to the Smyrnaeans* written by Ignatius, bishop of Antioch, who was being taken to Rome for execution. He had been a disciple of the apostle John. Constantine legalized Christianity much later, in 325.

b. The Church was called "Catholic" from the earliest times, long before Catholics could be found in most of the world. The universality of the Church refers not to her geographic extent but to her purpose: she is meant for everyone, everywhere.

c. The "birthday" of the Church is Pentecost, not the Ascension.

d. This is the correct, if unlikely-looking, answer. The Church is perfect not in her members—each of whom is a sinner and therefore imperfect—but "according to her nature and her rights [since] she possess in herself and by herself, by the will and the goodness of her Founder, everything that is necessary for her existence and her efficacy" (Pope Leo XIII, *Immortale Dei*, 1885).

e. The right answer is right above.

67

The first Christian emperor of the Roman Empire was

   a. Constantine, although he was baptized only at the end of his life.

   b. Theodosius, who made Christianity the state religion.

   c. Diocletian, who retired to what is now Split, Croatia, where his palace still stands.

   d. Minimaximus, who became a Christian at the end of the third century.

   e. none of the above.

a. Constantine legalized Christianity in his Edict of Milan, issued in 313. This did not establish Christianity as the state religion. It merely permitted Christians to practice their faith openly and without repression. The edict effectively ended the persecutions of Christianity by the Roman state. While Constantine seems to have accepted Christian beliefs, he was not baptized until shortly before his death in 337. He thus became, formally, a Christian in the final days of his reign and so counts as the first Christian emperor.

b. Theodosius reigned as Roman emperor from 379 to 395. In 380 he issued the Edict of Thessalonica, which declared that Catholicism, and not any heretical offshoot of it, was the legitimate imperial religion. In the process he ended state support for traditional Roman religions.

c. Far from being a Christian emperor, Diocletian arguably was the fiercest persecutor of the Church during the first three centuries of Christianity's existence. He did retire to Split, where his palace, largely intact, is at the center of the city.

d. There never was an emperor named Minimaximus. The name is made up.

e. The correct answer is *a*.

68

Which is *not* an attribute of God?

    a. omnipresence
    b. omniscience
    c. omnivorousness
    d. omnipotence
    e. none of the above

a. Omnipresence is the property of being everywhere. "Do I not fill heaven and earth? says the LORD" (Jer 23:24). "Yet he is not far from each one of us, for 'In him we live and move and have our being'" (Acts 17:27–28). In the Middle Ages theologians determined that God is omnipresent according to power, according to knowledge, and according to essence. For example, he is present in each created thing because he keeps each thing in being. Were he to withdraw himself and thus his superintendence, a thing would be annihilated. It would cease to be.

b. Omniscience is the property of knowing everything. God knows all things in the past, present, and future. "Before the universe was created, it was known to him; so it was also after it was finished" (Sir 23:20).

c. Omnivorousness is the property of being able to eat both animals and vegetables. Man has this property, but God doesn't, since he doesn't eat.

d. Omnipotence is the property of being all-powerful. "With God all things are possible" (Mt 19:26).

e. The correct answer is *c*.

69

Who were the first to establish that the existence of God can be known through reason alone, apart from revelation?

    a. ancient Greek (pagan) philosophers

    b. the Fathers of the Church (first through fourth centuries A.D.)

    c. Thomas Aquinas and other medieval theologians

    d. It is not true that God's existence can be known by reason alone; faith also is necessary.

    e. none of the above

a. Right. Preeminent among the Greek philosophers were Plato and Aristotle, who used reason to demonstrate that God exists.

b. Although many of the Fathers of the Church—the earliest Christian writers—argued in favor of God's existence and his attributes, they hardly were the first to do so. The earlier Greeks got there before them, even if they worked under the disadvantage of not having Christian revelation to aid in their considerations.

c. Thomas Aquinas is famous for giving five arguments for God's existence, but he lived in the thirteenth century and so could not have been the first to demonstrate that God's existence can be established through reason apart from revelation.

d. Faith is not required to establish God's existence. This is why it is possible for those without the virtue of faith to prove that God exists. They use reason alone, which is sufficient.

e. The first answer is the right answer.

70

How many judgments are there?

 a. None. Jesus taught, "Judge not, that you be not judged" (Mt 7:1).

 b. one, which occurs at death

 c. two, which occur at death and at the end of time

 d. three, which occur at death, on leaving purgatory, and at the end of time

 e. none of the above

a. When he said, "Judge not, that you be not judged", Jesus was not referring to any final judgments by God, which come after death, but to human judgments about things that cannot be known about other persons, such as their spiritual state.

b. There is a judgment by God that occurs at death, called the particular judgment. It determines whether a particular individual eventually ends up in heaven or in hell, but it is not the only post-death judgment.

c. The second post-death judgment will occur at the end of time. It is known as the general judgment. "[T]he Son of Man is to come with his angels in the glory of his Father, and then he will repay every man for what he has done" (Mt 16:27).

d. There is no judgment associated with leaving purgatory. Everyone who enters purgatory eventually will leave it for heaven, so there is no need for an additional judgment.

e. Answer *c* is correct.

71

According to the Bible, "without _____ it is impossible to please God" (cf. Heb 11:6).

    a. effort

    b. solitude

    c. hope

    d. fortitude

    e. none of the above

a. Certainly effort is needed, at least in the sense of cooperation with God's grace, but that is not the term found in the quotation.

b. Solitude can be helpful in recollecting one's thoughts and in turning them toward God, but solitude is not a precondition for pleasing God. There are many people who please God but who seldom or never have a chance to find themselves in true solitude.

c. Hope is one of the three theological virtues, but, again, it is not the word we are looking for.

d. Fortitude is one of the four cardinal virtues, the others being prudence, justice, and temperance. It is a high virtue, but it is not the word that goes in the blank.

e. The correct response is faith; therefore this is the right answer.

72

The Fourth Lateran Council (1215) called God "incomprehensible". This means

a. we can know nothing about God.

b. we can know everything about God.

c. we can know some things about God but not everything.

d. we can know nothing about God outside of what has been revealed.

e. none of the above.

a. In colloquial usage, we say something is incomprehensible if it is very confusing or if we can't seem to understand anything about it. This is not the meaning of the term in theology. When Lateran IV called God "incomprehensible", it didn't mean that we can't know anything about him.

b. One thing we should know is that it is impossible to know everything about God. That suggests that by calling God incomprehensible, we can't mean that it is possible to know him completely.

c. We can know some things about God through reason alone—for example, that he exists, created us, and rules the world. Other things we know about God only through revelation from God—for example, the Trinity (God's own inner life), the Hypostatic Union, and the Incarnation. But there is far more that we don't know about God and, given our creaturely limitations, can't know about him.

d. Wrong. We can know some things about God, such as the fact that he exists, through reason alone.

e. Answer *c* is correct.

73

Which of these ancient heretics are described properly?

    a. Arians denied that Christ had a human nature.

    b. Antipatrians taught that the Father was the least powerful Person of the Trinity.

    c. Pneumatomachians held that the Holy Spirit was the preeminent divine Person.

    d. Ebionites denied the divinity of Christ.

    e. none of the above

a. Quite the opposite. Arianism—named after Arius (c. 250–336), a priest in Alexandria, Egypt—held that the Son of God did not always exist but was created by the Father. Therefore, Jesus Christ was not God but a creature. He had a human nature but not a divine nature.

b. Although there may have been ancient heretics who thought this, there was no heretical group known as the Antipatrians.

c. The Pneumatomachians (also known as Macedonians) were fourth- and fifth-century heretics who denied the divinity of the Holy Spirit. The Greek name *Pneumatomachi* means "fighters against the Spirit". The founder of the heresy was Macedonius, who twice was bishop of Constantinople in the fourth century.

d. The Ebionites were Jewish Christians of the earliest centuries who thought Jesus was the Messiah, but they rejected his divinity and insisted that the old Jewish customary laws had to be followed. What little is known about them comes not so much from their own time as from later writings by patristic writers.

e. Answer *d* is correct.

74

Creation occurred

- a. because God was tired of being alone and wanted to give his love to creatures.
- b. through the instrumentality of a demiurge.
- c. out of nothing by the Logos, who was in all respects a creature.
- d. at a definite time that is calculable from dates given in the Old Testament.
- e. none of the above

a. God never lacks, and never has lacked, anything. Thus, he never could have felt loneliness. He brought our world into being not because he wanted companionship but so as to manifest his boundless love.

b. In some ancient belief systems, including some Christian heresies, the demiurge is a creature, lower than God but higher than other creatures, that is tasked with bringing the world into existence. Some scenarios posit a long line of demiurges, each giving existence to a lesser demiurge, with the lowest demiurge creating our world. There are two chief problems with such thinking. First, God himself created everything, with no need for intermediaries, and so demiurges don't exist. Second, a demiurge would be itself a creature, and no creature is capable of the act of creation—that is, of bringing something into being out of nothing. Only God can accomplish that.

c. The Logos (which means the "Word") is Jesus Christ. He is not a creature, except in his human nature. He is a divine Person who is himself the Creator.

d. Over the centuries people have tried to calculate when creation occurred by tallying dates and lifetimes given in the Bible. The most famous such person was James Ussher (1581–1656), the archbishop of Armagh for the (Protestant) Church of Ireland. According to his calculations, creation occurred on October 23, 4004 B.C. Ussher's chronology is sometimes used by today's young-Earth creationists, but otherwise it is given no credence. Among other famous men who tried to pinpoint the time of creation were the Venerable Bede (3952 B.C.), Johannes Kepler (3992 B.C.), and Isaac Newton (c. 4000 B.C.).

e. This is the right answer because the others are wrong.

75

The sin of our First Parents was disobedience, and the root of their disobedience was which of the following?

   a. lust
   b. fear of the Lord
   c. ambition
   d. sloth
   e. none of the above

a. There is no indication in Scripture that lust was involved.

b. Proverbs 9:10 says, "The fear of the Lord is the beginning of wisdom." It is not a sin but a gift of the Holy Spirit. Fear of the Lord is not the fear of punishment but the desire not to offend God.

c. The serpent told Eve that if she eats of the tree in the middle of the garden, her eyes "will be opened" and she "will be like God, knowing good and evil". Eve saw that the fruit was "to be desired to make one wise"—which is something she wanted—so "she took of its fruit and ate; and she also gave some to her husband, and he ate" (Gen 3:5–6). The two of them wanted to gain wisdom, wanted to know good and evil, and wanted to be like God. They were ambitious, out of pride, so this is the right answer.

d. In everyday usage, sloth means physical laziness, but in religion it means spiritual laziness, neglecting the things of God and being careless in one's religious duties. There is no reference to sloth in the story of Adam and Eve.

e. Answer *c* is correct.

76

How are angels organized into species?

   a. According to Thomas Aquinas, all angels together form one species.

   b. According to Albert the Great, each of the nine choirs of angels is a separate species.

   c. According to Francisco Suarez, each angel forms a separate species.

   d. According to Rodrigo Bellarmine, it makes no sense to refer to angels in terms of species because only plants and animals are categorized into species.

   e. none of the above

a. Thomas Aquinas (1225–1274) taught that each angel is a separate species. This is a conclusion he reached using the principle of individuation, the application of which results in the idea that each angel is specifically distinguished from every other angel.

b. It was Albert the Great (1193 / 1206–1280), not Aquinas, who taught that all angels form a single species, much as all men form a single species.

c. Francisco Suarez (1548–1617) is commonly regarded as one of the greatest Scholastic philosophers and theologians after Aquinas. He taught that each of the nine choirs of angels form a separate species. (The division of angels into nine choirs is not a truth of the faith but a theological speculation.)

d. There is no Saint Rodrigo Bellarmine. If you chose this answer, you might have been thinking of Robert Bellarmine (1542–1621).

e. Right, because all the other answers are wrong.

77

Which sacraments can be received only once?

    a. matrimony and baptism

    b. anointing of the sick and holy orders

    c. baptism, final vows, and holy orders

    d. confirmation, baptism, and holy orders

    e. none of the above

a. On the death of one's spouse, the sacrament of matrimony may be received again. In theory there is no limit to how many times this can be done, but in practice a multiplicity of marriages, even if sacramentally valid, will raise the suspicions of the public authorities.

b. Anointing of the sick may be received whenever there is danger of death or there is serious illness.

c. Finals vows are taken by men and women religious, but taking vows is not a sacrament.

d. Each of these sacraments may be received only once (for holy orders, only once at each level: deacon, priest, bishop), because each leaves an indelible mark on the soul. Remember the saying: "Once a priest, always a priest." Likewise with baptism and confirmation: once baptized or confirmed, always baptized or confirmed.

e. Answer *d* is correct.

78

What is the Hypostatic Union?

    a. the merging of Christ's divine and human wills into a perfected human will

    b. the existence in Christ of a perfect divine Person and a perfect human person

    c. the union of the Second Person's immaterial divine nature with Jesus' human nature, making a single perfected nature

    d. the union of the Western and Eastern Churches, destroyed at the Great Schism of 1054

    e. none of the above

a. The Hypostatic Union refers to the union of Christ's two natures. It is not about his two wills. In any case, his two wills do not become one. They remain distinct but in perfect harmony, the human will perfectly "synched" with the divine will.

b. Nor is the Hypostatic Union about Christ's personhood as such. In him there are not two persons but one, the divine.

c. This answer is closer but still wrong. The Hypostatic Union concerns the union of Christ's two natures, but the union is one in which those natures remain distinct from one another. The union doesn't result in a "single perfected nature", which, presumably, would have to be the divine nature.

d. The Hypostatic Union is a teaching about Christology, not about ecclesiology.

e. None of the above answers is correct, so this one is.

79

What is a miracle?

a. an occurrence that seems to contradict scientific laws but really does not

b. any unexplained occurrence that includes a spiritual element

c. an ancient explanation in lieu of modern scientific knowledge

d. a pious story that helps us understand religious truth without being true itself

e. none of the above

a. Tossing out this proposed definition is easy: just think of any miracle recorded in the New Testament, such as the Resurrection, which certainly contradicted the scientific law (if it may be put this way) of "once dead, always dead".

b. This is too vague. Probably everyone has lived through unexplained occurrences that include some spiritual elements, such as witnessing a spectacular but unexplainable atmospheric occurrence, at the sight of which one's mind is lifted toward God. That's a fine thing, but it's not a miracle.

c. This is the common allegation of nonbelievers: miracles are answers provided by primitive people who didn't know much about science or medicine. Yet miracles continue to occur, such as those rigorously vetted during the canonization processes for modern saints. Such miracles are examined by highly trained scientists and physicians who deliberately use modern scientific knowledge in their investigations.

d. A miracle is not itself a story, though there are stories about miracles, just as any historical event is not itself a story, though there may be stories about it.

e. None of the above answers is correct, so this one is.

80

Which answer includes one or two sins that are *not* among the seven deadly sins?

- a. anger and wrath
- b. peevishness and lust
- c. greed and avarice
- d. pride and envy
- e. none of the above

a. Anger and wrath are two words for the same sin, which is one of the seven deadlies.

b. Correct. While lust is one of the seven deadly sins, peevishness is not.

c. Again we have synonyms: greed and avarice are the same deadly sin.

d. Pride and envy are two of the deadly sins, with pride generally being considered the worst of them all.

e. The correct answer is *b*.

81

The human soul

   a. becomes at death an angelic spirit.

   b. is a simple substance.

   c. is composed of an infinite number of parts and therefore can extend throughout space.

   d. is the same as an animal soul except that it is immortal.

   e. none of the above

a. Angels and men are quite different creatures. Angels are pure spirits, period. Men are both spirits (souls) and matter (bodies). The human spirit is similar to the angelic spirit in that it is immortal, but otherwise the two are distinct. When someone dies, his soul separates from his body and exists on its own until the resurrection of the body at the end of time, but it exists as a human soul, not as an angel.

b. This is the right answer. When we say the human soul is a simple substance, we don't mean that understanding it is simple, nor do we mean that the human soul is a *material* substance. We are using a philosophic term that means that the human soul is not made of parts. This is true of every spirit, and this simplicity is why spirits can't die. Our bodies, in contrast, are made of parts, countless numbers of them, right down to the subatomic level. When we die, our bodies fall apart; they cease to be unities. This can't happen to spirits.

c. Just the opposite: souls have no parts because they are spirits.

d. The human soul is a spirit, but the soul of an animal is not. An animal's soul dies when the animal dies. The human soul, being a spirit, doesn't die when the body dies.

e. Answer *b* is correct.

82

When a property or activity of God that is common among the three Persons is attributed to an individual Person, it is called which of the following?

a. division of labor
b. separation of powers
c. appropriation
d. analogy
e. none of the above

a. This is a good principle in the business world, but it doesn't apply to theology.

b. The U.S. Constitution provides for a separation of powers among the three branches of government: executive, legislative, and judicial. It is a good arrangement, but it doesn't mirror what occurs within the Trinity.

c. Right. Appropriation is the attributing of names, qualities, or operations to one of the three Persons of the Trinity without excluding the other two. For example, we normally consider omnipotence to be an attribute of the Father (which it is), but the Son and the Holy Spirit are omnipotent also. When we think of wisdom, we might think more of the Son or of the Holy Spirit, but all three Persons are equally wise. We associate love with the Holy Spirit, but we know that the Father and the Son love equally. This equality of attributes arises from the fact that the three Persons have one nature and therefore must be equal in omnipotence, wisdom, and love.

d. An analogy is a comparison between two things that are in some way similar, but analogy is not relevant to the issue given above.

e. The correct answer is *c*.

83

Who were the Montanists?

   a. an ancient sect that promoted moral laxity

   b. a second-century movement of those who said it was obligatory to make a pilgrimage to Mount Sinai, the movement's name deriving from *mons*, the Latin word for mountain

   c. followers of Montanus, bishop of Constantinople in the fifth century

   d. followers of female visionaries named Prisca and Maximilla

   e. none of the above

a. Quite the opposite. Montanists were noted for their moral and ethical rigor, at least in certain areas. They forbade remarriage after the death of a spouse, for example, and they insisted on strict and frequent fasting.

b. This answer is entirely fanciful, except in terms of dating: Montanism was a heresy of the late second century, but it had nothing to do with Mount Sinai, and its name derived from the name of its founder, Montanus.

c. There was no bishop of Constantinople by the name of Montanus.

d. Prisca (also known as Priscilla) and Maximilla were colleagues of Montanus. Some scholars consider them to be cofounders of Montanism. They were known for ecstatic visions and achieved wide followings. Thus, it is proper to say that Montanists were followers not just of Montanus but of Prisca and Maximilla.

e. Answer *d* is correct.

84

Which pope was a significant figure during the Counter-Reformation?

    a. Sixtus V

    b. Fiftus VI

    c. Sylvester IV

    d. Pius VII

    e. none of the above

a. Not a particularly likable man, Sixtus V (reigned 1585–1590) accomplished much during his short pontificate, which occurred during the Counter-Reformation. Under his direction many architectural projects were completed in Rome, including the dome of Saint Peter's and repairs to the Quirinal, Lateran, and Vatican Palaces. He limited the College of Cardinals to seventy members and increased the number of Vatican congregations in order to make the bureaucracy function more efficiently.

b. There never were any popes named Fiftus, let alone six of them.

c. There were three popes named Sylvester, the last reigning for a short time in 1045, long before the Counter-Reformation. There was, though, an anti-pope called Sylvester IV (died 1111).

d. Pius VII was pope from 1800 to 1823, long after the conclusion of the Counter-Reformation. During the first fifteen years of his papacy, Pius had much difficulty with Napoleon; when the French armies occupied the Papal States in 1809, he was taken prisoner and exiled to Savona. After the United States succeeded in defeating the Barbary Pirates, thus ending the kidnapping of Christians for ransom and slavery, Pius said that the United States "had done more for the cause of Christianity than the most powerful nations of Christendom have done for ages".

e. The correct answer is *a*.

85

Before the Fall, Adam and Eve

   a. enjoyed freedom from all bodily suffering but not from emotional suffering.

   b. enjoyed immortality, a consequence of which was that they could not sin.

   c. did not understand that God was their Creator; they learned this only after first sinning.

   d. had a full understanding of their premortal lives in heaven.

   e. none of the above

a. Adam and Eve enjoyed not just freedom from physical suffering, such as illness, but freedom from every other kind of suffering as well. They lost this freedom at the Fall.

b. They did have the gift of immortality, meaning both body and soul would live forever, but they lost it when they sinned. Likewise, angels have the gift of immortality, but that did not prevent some of them from sinning.

c. There is nothing in Genesis to suggest that Adam and Eve did not realize who God was.

d. There is no such thing as a premortal life, in other words, the existence of the soul in heaven before being infused into a body. This is contrary to the teaching that God creates each human soul at the moment of conception.

e. Since all four answers above are wrong, this one is right.

86

What are the four marks of the Church?

   a. Saint Mark the Martyr, Pope Saint Mark, Saint Mark Chrysostom, and Saint Mark the Evangelist

   b. holiness, catholicity, universality, apostolicity

   c. sacraments, sacramentals, pious devotions, and rosaries

   d. pope, cardinal, bishop, and priest

   e. none of the above

a. There is no saint known as Mark the Martyr. There was one pope named Mark; he reigned for fewer than eight months in 336. The saint who was given the epithet Chrysostom (golden mouthed) because of his eloquent preaching was named John, not Mark, and lived from about 347 to 407. Neither Mark the Evangelist nor any of these other Marks ranks as one of the four marks of the Church.

b. The four marks of the Church are found in the Creed, where we affirm our belief in "one, holy, catholic, and apostolic Church". The listing here almost is correct, but the Church's unity is left out, and catholicity is the same thing as universality.

c. Four good things but quite distinct from the four marks.

d. These are four levels of priestly authority in the Church, but they are not what is meant by the four marks.

e. Each of the above answers is incorrect, making this one the right answer.

87

In terms of religion, what is a mystery?

   a. a story with an unexpected ending

   b. something contrary to reason but not contrary to faith

   c. a religious truth that we cannot know everything about

   d. There are no mysteries in the Catholic faith since everything can be understood from the *Catechism of the Catholic Church*.

   e. none of the above

a. The term *mystery* has multiple meanings. Perhaps the most widespread nowadays is that of the mystery story or detective story, but that is a secular, not a religious, meaning.

b. A mystery is a religious truth about which we would know nothing unless it had been revealed to us—that is, we never could reason to it on our own. Among the mysteries are the Hypostatic Union, the Eucharist, and the Trinity. While we accept a mystery on faith (on the word of Christ, who revealed the mystery to us), there is nothing contrary to reason within the mystery itself.

c. While a mystery is a religious truth, it is not one about which we can know everything, the way we can know everything about the multiplication table. A mystery is a truth about which we know something (because it has been revealed to us by Christ) and concerning which we can draw true inferences and deductions, yet a mystery remains fundamentally beyond the capacity of the human mind to comprehend fully.

d. This answer uses the term *mysteries* to mean things that are confusing or that can't be understood at all, but that is not the theological meaning. The *Catechism of the Catholic Church* explains Church teachings in considerable detail, and it defines *mysteries* as given in answer *c*.

e. Answer *c* is correct.

88

Who designed the dome of the cathedral of Florence?

a. Michelangelo Buonarroti

b. Giovanni Lorenzo Bernini

c. Filippo Brunelleschi

d. Lorenzo Ghiberti

e. none of the above

a. Good guess, but no. Michelangelo (1475–1564) is famous for having designed the dome of Saint Peter's Basilica in Rome, not that of the Basilica of Santa Maria del Fiore (Saint Mary of the Flower) in Florence.

b. Bernini (1598–1680) was a prominent artist and architect and the foremost sculptor of his time, but he came along far too late to work on the Duomo, as Florence's cathedral commonly is called. Its construction was finished in 1469 with the placing of a copper ball atop the dome's lantern.

c. Brunelleschi (1377–1446) managed the remarkable feat of constructing the gigantic octagonal dome. At the time—work started on the dome in 1420—no one knew how such a dome could be constructed without using a massive and infeasible amount of wooden scaffolding. Brunelleschi used a complex herringbone pattern for the four million bricks that were used in building the dome, and he invented machines to hoist the bricks to great heights.

d. Ghiberti (1378–1455) was Brunelleschi's longtime competitor. In 1401 they participated in a competition to see which artist would get the commission to design a set of bronze doors for the Florence Baptistery. Ghiberti won. They competed again in 1418 for the commission to design the dome, and that time Brunelleschi won.

e. The correct answer is *c*.

89

How do we know which books belong in the Bible?

   a. by referring to the table of contents

   b. The books demonstrate their canonicity through their evident lofty style.

   c. through ancient decrees of the Catholic Church

   d. by the common consent of all major Christian bodies

   e. none of the above

a. Although tables of contents can be found in antiquity—Quintus Valerius Soranus (died 82 B.C.) is said to be the first author to provide a table of contents for one of his lengthy works—the Bible's table of contents came into use centuries after the sacred books were written and the canon was finalized. Thus, the table of contents can be of no help in deciding which books belong in the Bible.

b. To many people, some books of the Bible seem, in their writing, to be pedestrian. This is particularly the case with books such as Deuteronomy and Numbers, with their ceremonial and dietary regulations. If canonicity were determined by literary style, would that mean that dull or dry passages would have to be stricken from the sacred texts?

c. Right. The canon of the Bible was determined by early Church councils, such as those held at Hippo in 393 and at Carthage in 397.

d. Unfortunately, when it comes to the canon of the Bible, there is no common consent of all major Christian bodies. Catholics and Eastern Orthodox agree on a Bible comprising seventy-three books, while most Protestants say the Bible has only sixty-six books.

e. Answer *c* is correct.

90

Which of these is not one of the seven gifts of the Holy Spirit?

a. fortitude
b. piety
c. chastity
d. knowledge
e. none of the above

a. Fortitude is one of the seven gifts of the Holy Spirit, the others being wisdom, understanding, counsel, knowledge, piety, and fear of the Lord (in the sense of wonder or awe, not in the sense of being frightened of him). The origin of the list is found in Isaiah 11:2.

b. Piety is another gift of the Holy Spirit.

c. Nope. Chastity isn't listed among the seven gifts of the Holy Spirit. It is one of seven virtues that are opposed to the seven deadly sins: chastity versus lust, temperance versus gluttony, charity versus greed, diligence versus sloth, patience versus wrath, kindness versus envy, and humility versus pride.

d. Knowledge is another gift of the Holy Spirit.

e. Answer *c* is correct.

91

Which of these will be occupied eternally?

    a. heaven, purgatory, and hell
    b. heaven, hell, and the limbo of the Fathers
    c. only hell
    d. only heaven, as the others will end at the *apokatastasis*
    e. none of the above

a. Heaven and hell are eternal, and each will have occupants. (We know some of them for certain: the saints and good angels in heaven, the bad angels in hell.) Everyone who goes to purgatory has died in the state of grace and eventually will get to heaven, which means that in the end there will be two occupied "places".

b. The limbo of the Fathers is that state or place to which Christ descended after his death on the cross. It was there that he preached to the spirits in prison (1 Pet 3:19), holy people, such as the patriarchs and prophets, who had died in earlier times and who waited for heaven to be opened at Christ's Resurrection. If this limbo of the Fathers was the same place as purgatory, then see answer *a*. If it was a separate state or place, then it was emptied once heaven was opened.

c. That may be Satan's wish, but heaven will be equally eternal.

d. The Greek word *apokatastasis* means "restoration". It is used for the theological speculation that, at some undetermined point, the damned will be released from hell and will enter heaven, their punishment having been concluded. It is an idea most commonly associated with the third-century writer Origen and is a species of universalism. The speculation is not compatible with Catholic teaching, which holds that both heaven and hell are eternal.

e. None of the above answers is correct, so this one is.

92

When the Catholic Church is described as holy, it means that

    a. none of her members sins grievously.

    b. she has produced more saints than has any other religious body.

    c. she holds up holiness as an ideal that can be approached but never reached.

    d. she is holy in her origins and purposes, no matter how bad some of her members may be.

    e. none of the above

a. If this were true, it would mean that no Catholic ever commits mortal sins. That would be wonderful, but we know from our own lives and from observing the lives of other Catholics that this just isn't so.

b. Although the Catholic Church has produced saintly people, that is not what is meant when we say the Church is holy—though it is a consequence of the Church's holiness.

c. While the perfect holiness of God never can be reached, nor even the preeminent holiness of the Virgin Mary (the holiest of all creatures), holiness is achievable by anyone. Every saint in heaven is holy and is there only because every imperfection has been wrung out of him, either on Earth or in purgatory. The Church constantly urges us to greater degrees of holiness, but even lesser degrees can be reached by "regular" Catholics.

d. Correct. The Catholic Church is holy in her origins in that she was founded by God himself (Mt 16:18–19), and she is holy in her purposes because her chief purpose is to inculcate holiness in her members so they can live eternally in heaven with God.

e. Answer *d* is correct.

93

The unity of the Church

    a. was lost when the Protestants broke away in the sixteenth century, because they did away with the priesthood.

    b. was lost when the Eastern Orthodox broke away in the eleventh century, even though they maintained all seven sacraments

    c. is a perpetual attribute of the Church and has nothing to do with how many groups break away.

    d. is an ideal toward which all Christians need to work together.

    e. none of the above

a. We have to distinguish between the unity of Christians and the unity that is a hallmark of the Church. The unity of the Church—understood as one of her four marks—remains even when groups split off from the Church. See answer *c*.

b. This is a variant of answer *a* and is equally wrong.

c. Unity is one of the four marks of the Church. By *unity* is meant that Christ established only one Church, and there remains only one true Church. All other Christian bodies are offshoots of that Church; many of them are offshoots of offshoots. These bodies maintain some elements of the one Church, such as (in most cases) valid baptisms and authentic (if usually truncated) versions of Sacred Scripture, but they are not, properly speaking, parts of the Church founded by Christ.

d. Since the unity of the Church, in the sense given above, always has existed and is in no way impaired, it makes no sense to speak of working toward it as an ideal, but it does make sense to speak of working toward the unification of all Christians with one another. This would be accomplished most perfectly if all Christians belonged to the one Church Christ established, which is the Catholic Church.

e. Answer *c* is correct.

94

Who was the first pope to write a social encyclical?

a. John Paul II (*Summorum Pontificum* in 1979)

b. John XXII (*Mater et Magistra* in 1961)

c. Leo XIII (*Sensus Fidelium* in 1891)

d. Pius IX (*Rerum Novarum* in 1896)

e. none of the above

a. *Summorum Pontificum* is a noteworthy document, but it's not a social encyclical. It's not an encyclical at all. It's the apostolic letter, issued in 2007, through which Benedict XVI (not John Paul II) set out regulations for the wider use of the Latin Mass using the 1962 missal. This form of the Mass commonly is called the Extraordinary Form.

b. *Mater et Magistra* indeed is a social encyclical. It was issued in observance of the seventieth anniversary of the first social encyclical, *Rerum Novarum*, which appeared in 1891.

c. There never has been an encyclical with this title. *Sensus fidelium* means "the sense of the faithful" and refers to the body of Catholics as a whole when, " 'from the Bishops down to the last of the lay faithful' they show universal agreement in matters of faith and morals" (*Lumen gentium*, 12, quoting Saint Augustine).

d. *Rerum Novarum* is the right encyclical, but the year is wrong—it should be 1891—and the pope is wrong. The encyclical was issued by Leo XIII, not by Pius IX, who had died in 1878.

e. By process of elimination, this is the correct answer.

95

The Lateran Treaty

   a. established the basilica of Saint John Lateran as the cathedral of the Diocese of Rome.

   b. was signed by Benito Mussolini and Pope Pius XI in 1929.

   c. was the concluding document of the most important ecumenical council of the Middle Ages, Lateran IV (1215).

   d. set up the European Union, of which Vatican City is a member state.

   e. none of the above

a. The basilica of Saint John Lateran was dedicated, in its original form, in 324. It is named after Saints John the Evangelist and John the Baptist. The word *Lateran* indicates that the property on which the basilica stands once was owned by the Lateranus family, which lost its properties to the emperor Constantine; he gave them to the Church in 311. The Lateran Treaty was signed 1,605 years after the basilica became Rome's cathedral.

b. It is true that the Lateran Treaty was signed in 1929. It was one of several simultaneously signed documents that set the relationship between the Italian state and the Catholic Church. One result was the establishment of Vatican City State as an independent country. Mussolini was the head of the Italian government, and Pius XI was the pope. Mussolini signed the documents, but Pius didn't. It was Cardinal Pietro Gasparri (1852–1934) who signed on behalf of the Church, in his role as secretary of state of the Vatican.

c. Right location, wrong document.

d. The European Union's founding treaties are the Treaty on European Union (also called the Maastricht Treaty, 1993) and the Treaty on the Functioning of the European Union (also called the Treaty of Rome, 1958). Although Italy is a member of the European Union, Vatican City State is not.

e. The other four answers are wrong.

96

Faithful Catholics must believe in the following apparitions:

a. Lourdes, because of the large number of proven miraculous cures there

b. Fátima, because the miracle of the sun was witnessed by seventy thousand people, and their testimony is conclusive

c. Guadalupe, because it was followed by the rapid spread of Catholicism in Mexico

d. Lourdes, Fátima, and Guadalupe

e. none of the above

a. There is good reason to believe that miraculous cures have occurred at Lourdes, particularly given the skepticism and precision employed at the Lourdes Medical Bureau, but no one is obligated to believe that there really was an apparition at Lourdes or even that anyone has been cured there.

b. As with Lourdes, so with Fátima. The testimony of a great many witnesses to an event may be enough to convince someone that the event really occurred, but the Church demands of the faithful no such belief.

c. In some ways the conversion of Mexico can be considered more remarkable than the cures of Lourdes or the miracle of the sun at Fátima, but even that grand historical fact does not compel Catholics to believe that there was a true apparition at Guadalupe.

d. If there is no obligation to subscribe to any of these private apparitions, there can be no obligation to subscribe to all three of them.

e. None of the above answers is correct because Catholics never are obliged to believe in any particular private apparition, so this one is.

97

Souls in purgatory

    a. can be assisted by the intercession of Catholics but not of Protestants.

    b. are unable to intercede for those on Earth.

    c. will remain in purgatory until the Last Day.

    d. exist in a state of suspended animation until released to heaven

    e. none of the above

a. The ecumenical councils of Second Lyon (1274) and Florence (1439) taught that souls in purgatory can benefit from the Mass and from "prayers and alms and other works of piety, which the faithful are accustomed to perform for one another according to the institutions of the Church". There is no restriction on the doer: if anyone, Catholic or Protestant, were to pray for someone who may be in purgatory, the prayer would be effective.

b. Souls in purgatory remain members of the Mystical Body of Christ. Just as we can pray for them, they can pray for us. In 1889 Pope Leo XIII ratified an indulgenced prayer in which the souls in purgatory are asked to pray for the ill. This prayer later was dropped from collections of indulgenced prayers, but, as theologian Ludwig Ott pointed out, the "permissibility of such invocation is not to be doubted" (*Fundamentals of Catholic Dogma*, Tan Books, 1974, p. 323).

c. Souls leave purgatory and enter heaven when they have satisfied the temporal punishment due to sin and when they have been cleansed of any remaining affection for sin, no matter how small. There is no requirement that they remain in purgatory until the Last Day.

d. By "suspended animation" most people understand a state of absolute inactivity and mental vacuousness or unconsciousness. This is not at all the condition of the dead, no matter where they may be.

e. This is the correct answer because each of the others is wrong.

98

The sacraments

a. contain the grace they signify and bestow it on the recipients of the sacraments, regardless of their dispositions.

b. work *ex opere operato*, which means that their efficacy depends on the holiness of those administering them.

c. all confer the same kind of grace.

d. were established by the Church at the first-century Council of Jerusalem.

e. none of the above

a. It is true that sacraments signify and confer grace, but the conferral is not automatic or in spite of the dispositions of the intended recipients. You won't have your sins forgiven when the priest absolves you in the confessional, for example, if you don't *want* your sins to be forgiven or if you aren't truly sorry for them. Similarly, an adult could undergo baptism outwardly, with water being poured on him while the proper words are recited ("I baptize you in the name of the Father, and of the Son, and of the Holy Spirit"), but the baptism won't be effective if he doesn't *want* to be baptized. (Thus, there is no such thing as a forced baptism, except in outward appearances.)

b. The efficacy of a sacrament is not dependent on the holiness of the person administering it. Someone in the state of mortal sin can perform a valid baptism, for example, and a priest in mortal sin can perform a valid Mass. The phrase *ex opere operato* means "from the work worked" and indicates that the efficacy of a sacrament is due to the sacrament's being performed, regardless of the merits or demerits of the person performing it.

c. Each sacrament confers a specific grace geared toward achieving the particular purpose of the sacrament.

d. All seven sacraments were instituted by Christ. This was taught formally by the Council of Trent against the position of the Protestant Reformers, who said that most of the sacraments were human inventions.

e. This is the correct answer.

99

Veneration of saints

- a. means giving them adoration in a lesser degree than the adoration given to God.
- b. is a phrase no longer used; we now say that we honor saints.
- c. is what Orestes Brownson meant by the word *worship* in his nineteenth-century book *Saint Worship*.
- d. was encouraged by the eighth ecumenical council, which met at Regensburg.
- e. none of the above

a. Adoration is reserved to God alone.

b. Some people say we honor saints, and others say we venerate saints. The terms are equivalent, and both remain in use.

c. This is true. As late as the nineteenth century the term *worship* included both adoration and veneration. Today it means adoration only. We still see a remnant of the older usage in Britain, where certain magistrates are addressed as "Your Worship". No one imagines that the people addressing the magistrates in this way are adoring them. In his thin book *Saint Worship*, Brownson, who was an American convert to Catholicism from Unitarianism, defended the veneration of saints against Protestant attacks.

d. The eighth ecumenical council, called the Fourth Council of Constantinople (869–870), took place, fairly obviously, in Constantinople. There never has been an ecumenical council in Regensburg, Germany.

e. The correct answer is *c*.

100

Which saint is properly paired with the group of which he is the patron?

   a. Francis de Sales and merchants

   b. Jane Frances de Chantal and singers of Gregorian chant

   c. Isidore of Seville and barbers and hairdressers

   d. Isabella of Castile and makers of soap

   e. none of the above

a. Francis (1567–1622) is called "de Sales" because he was born in the Château de Sales and into the noble Sales family in what then was the Duchy of Savoy but now is part of France. His name has nothing to do with his being a salesman—which he wasn't. He was the bishop of Geneva and had remarkable success in countering the Reformation there. He is the patron of writers, authors, and journalists.

b. Jane Frances de Chantal (1572–1641) had nothing to do with chanting, except to the extent that she and her nuns may have used chant in their convent. Jane was a friend of Francis de Sales, who was her spiritual director. She is the patroness of forgotten people, those with in-law problems, and parents separated from their children.

c. If you chose this answer, you probably had Gioacchino Rossini's opera *The Barber of Seville* at the back of your mind. Isidore (560–636) had nothing to do with barbers, except that he may have made use of the services of one while he served as archbishop of Seville. He is the patron of the Internet, computer users, computer programmers, and students.

d. Isabella (1451–1504) is best known to Americans for her underwriting of Christopher Columbus' 1492 voyage. She is not a canonized saint and therefore is not counted as a patroness—certainly not of soap. Her cause for canonization was begun in 1958 and continues. In 1974 she was given the title Servant of God.

e. Correct, because all the other possible answers are wrong.

HOW DO YOU RANK?

Fewer than 20 correct answers:

There is no word for this result other than pitiable. Random guessing should have given you one out of five correct answers, for a score of 20. I hardly know what to advise, other than that you should get a child's catechism, the *Catechism of the Catholic Church*, and books about saints and Church history—and then devote every free moment for the next six months to learning the rudiments of your faith. By that time you will have forgotten this quiz. Purchase a fresh copy of this book and try again. If you score equally poorly, throw yourself on the mercy of the divine court.

20 to 39 correct answers:

In school, such a result would have earned you an F, and I can give you nothing higher. You are not ranked among the near hopeless (see above), but you should not share your score with anyone whose esteem you wish to keep. Hit the books for the next few months, and try the quiz again. You likely will do much better. If you don't, consider becoming a hermit.

40 to 59 correct answers:

Not impressive, but nothing to be ashamed about. You will be spared public penance. You will be consoled to learn that most Catholics score in this range, even regular Mass goers who attended Catholic schools.

60 to 79 correct answers:

You soon will be able to take over the adult education classes in your parish. Your score is better than average, and it shouldn't take you long to fill the gaps in your knowledge. Take a look at which kinds of questions you got wrong—doctrine, history, morals, saints?—and study up in those areas.

80 to 99 correct answers:

You have done so well that you may be tempted to gloat over your accomplishment—but don't do that. It's unbecoming in someone with your smarts. Just take quiet satisfaction in knowing that you are among the very few who can score this high.

100 correct answers:

Magnificent! You should consider becoming a full-time Catholic apologist.